Slipcovers & Bedding

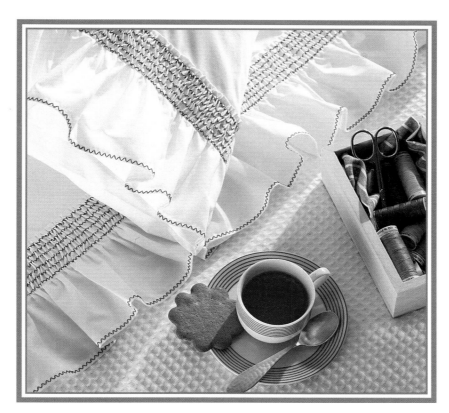

Front cover (l): Worldwide Syndication Ltd;
(tr): Elizabeth Whiting & Associates/Peter Woloszynski;
(br): Biggie Best Interiors (tel:+44 117-987-27-22).

Page 3: Eaglemoss/Lizzie Orme; page 5: Eaglemoss/Lizzie Orme;
page 6: Marie Claire Idées/F.Bouquet/C.Lancrenon;
page 7: Eaglemoss/Lizzie Orme; page 8: Eaglemoss/Steve Tanner.

First published in North America
in 1998 by Betterway Books
an imprint of F&W Publications Inc
1507 Dana Avenue
Cincinnati, Ohio 45207
1-800-289-0963

ISBN 1–55870–492–2

Manufactured in Spain

10 9 8 7 6 5 4 3 2 1

sew in a weekend

Slipcovers & Bedding

BETTERWAY BOOKS
Cincinnati, Ohio

Contents

1
Slipcovers

Slipcovers aren't just for hiding old sofas. Revamp a whole room –
from chairs to boxes to headboards – for a totally coordinated look
that's fresh, inexpensive and surprisingly easy to do

2
Bedding

Create the bed of your dreams without spending a fortune. Sewing your own bedding allows you to match new pieces to existing soft furnishings or create a whole new style that is completely your own

Fabrics for slipcovers

Slipcover fabrics need to be strong and hardwearing.
Learn what qualities to look for when you are choosing your fabric
and how to ensure that it meets fire safety requirements.

Fabrics used to cover seating are put under a lot of strain. Not only do you sit on the fabric and rub against it with your clothes, complete with buckles and zippers, but there are the everyday spills that can never be ruled out. Add to this the accumulation of dust and pet hairs, and you begin to realize why slipcover fabrics need to be particularly hardy.

Patterned fabrics

A patterned fabric – even one with a very small, unobtrusive pattern – has the advantage of showing marks and wear less than a plain fabric. It is also a good way of introducing a small amount of pattern into a room.

If you are considering using a larger pattern, it will need to be centred – on the seat or back of a chair, or on each cushion of a sofa, for example – so you need to buy extra fabric to allow for this. Check the pattern repeat widthways as well as lengthways, to see how you will position the motifs and whether additional fabric will be required. Also check that the pattern runs on the straight

▲ *Choose linen union for a fresh, natural look. Here, the simple, vertical stripes of the fabric complement the shape of the sofa, with its elegant spindle-legs.*

grain of the fabric. If it doesn't, this can be very noticeable – if the pattern runs out along the top of a sofa, say.

Choosing slipcover fabrics

If you want a fabric to last, don't skimp on the price. The following points will help you when choosing your fabric:

Flaws Look out for defects in the fabric construction – usually marked with a coloured tag on the selvedge. These will become weak points, where the fabric could split or wear more quickly.

Fibre content Many fabrics consist of a combination of fibres, both natural and synthetic. Bear the characteristics of the fibre in mind when considering whether the fabric is suitable for your furniture.

Weave The fabric should be firm and closely woven. Many fabrics are specially woven for upholstery, with more threads per inch than curtaining fabrics. Twill weaves, which have a diagonal line across the fabric, are more hardwearing than plain weaves.

Texture A textured fabric doesn't show wear and marks as much as a smooth one. Fabrics with long floats of thread on the surface may, however, catch and pull.

Colour In general, marks show up less on dark colours than on pale ones – but very dark, smooth fabrics can show some marks even more.

Popular upholstery fabrics

The following fabrics are durable enough for seating. If you are in any doubt as to a fabric's suitability, check with the supplier or manufacturer.

Furnishing cottons are available in plain colours (A), as well as a wide variety of printed patterns (B). There are many different textures – from the ribbed appearance of sample A, to cottons with a brushed or shiny surface. The fabric must have a close weave and be heavy enough for its intended purpose.

Linen union is a mixture of linen and cotton, or sometimes linen and jute; the addition of cotton or jute makes a tough fabric. Linen union is used in its undyed state (C) for a natural look, or printed (D) for a classic, country house look.

Heavy-duty chintzes (E) are suitable for upholstery which does not get very heavy wear. Chintz is often, although not necessarily, floral; its distinguishing characteristic is its glazed finish.

Tapestry (F) is a heavily textured, durable fabric, ideal for upholstery. It often features an elaborate, traditional design. Originally made from wool or silk, modern tapestries often contain viscose or other manmade fibres.

Pile fabrics are popular for seating, as they are warm and welcoming to the touch, as well as being hardwearing. **Plain velvet** (G) is luxurious, but can quickly look shabby, as the pile flattens in areas of constant use. Choose darker colours, or patterned or **figured velvet** (H) to minimize this problem. **Chenille** (I) has recently become popular for upholstery. For an intricately textured effect, chenille threads are woven with other yarns (J).

Woven motifs (K), sometimes called dobby weaves, add interest to a plain cloth and distract the eye from any defects or stains which may occur. A tiny motif is woven into the fabric, sometimes using a thicker thread, which adds strength.

Damasks and brocades are both highly patterned jacquard fabrics. **Damask** has a matt design on a satin ground; the warp and weft may be the same colour or contrasting (L). **Brocade** (M) is characterized by a raised pattern on one side and floats of thread on the other. Upholstery damasks and brocades are made from cotton, linen, wool, silk or synthetics – or from a blend of these.

Checks (N) **and stripes** look smart and fresh for upholstery, but must be used with care. It's hard to keep stripes running straight when you pull fabric tight – and checks are even more difficult to keep in line. Checks and stripes may be unsuitable for some furniture shapes, where there is deep buttoning or where fabric converges from different directions.

▲ *This stylish sofa is covered in a rich-looking damask. The gracefully curved, back cushions and the scroll-shaped arms are cleverly echoed in the curled motif of the fabric.*

Fabric care

Laundering

Loose covers must be dry cleaned to preserve the flame-retardant finish, unless the fabric is specified as being both flameproof and washable.

Tight covers can be treated with a stain-repellent to make the fabric less absorbent, so liquids remain on the surface for longer and can be mopped up before they can soak in. Either buy a spray or find a company which will visit your home to treat the fabric.

General cleaning

◆ Vacuum clean or brush with a soft brush, to keep dust out of the fibres and prolong the life of the fabric.

◆ Apply a carpet and upholstery shampoo to freshen up tired covers.

◆ Use a de-fluff mitt or a wet rubber glove to remove pet hairs.

◆ Mop up liquid spills with a sponge and tepid water. Leave dirt to dry, then remove with a toothbrush.

◆ Use a dry-cleaning spray to treat spot stains. The spray dries into a fine powder which is brushed off. Test in a corner of the furniture first.

Needles and stitches

◆ **Machine needles** Sizes 90/14 to 110/18

◆ **Stitch length** 3 to 3.5 millimetres (8 to 7 stitches per inch)

◆ **Hand needles** Betweens sizes 5 to 9 for slipstitching; a semi-circular needle for stitching fabric edges together on the furniture frame; a long needle for buttoning

◆ **Thread** Extra strong, extra upholstery or linen thread

◆ **Other tools** A selection of tools, such as a hammer and staple gun, are also needed

▶ *The sumptuous shape of this armchair calls for an appropriately luxurious fabric to cover it. Chenille, with its thick, velvety threads, is an ideal choice.*

▲ *This striking cotton fabric introduces a range of flame colours into the room – the broad stripes merging from one shade into the next. The seams are piped with self-fabric for extra definition.*

Sewing advice

The following tips will help you when sewing upholstery fabrics:

◆ **Cutting out** Cut out the pattern pieces exactly on the straight grain for maximum strength.

◆ **Layering and notching** Upholstery fabrics tend to be thicker than other fabrics, so reduce bulk to make stitching easier and give a smoother outline. Layer the seam allowances where one seam crosses another, and cut notches out of the seam allowances on outward curves.

◆ **Seams** Use flat-fell seams wherever possible on loose covers. Piping a seam helps to give more strength to the construction.

◆ **Pinning and tacking** Wobbly seams and badly matched patterns really show up when they are stretched taut, so pin and tack carefully before stitching.

Fire safety

The fumes from burning foam rubber are extremely toxic, so the foam must be treated to make it flame retardant. The fabric used to cover it is also subject to strict regulations, to guard against the danger of fire and the toxic fumes given off, should there be a fire.

Flame-retardant fabrics

Some upholstery fabrics come with built-in flame retardancy, to Match Test Standard. These fabrics are suitable for both tight and loose covers. (Fabric for loose covers *must* be flame retardant, since you cannot be certain that the furniture being covered does not contain foam.)

Using a barrier cloth

Other upholstery fabrics pass the Cigarette Test, but need a barrier cloth (also called flame-retardant interliner) underneath to bring them up to the required standard for tight covers. Flameproof barrier cloth is available from good fabric suppliers.

Covered furniture made before 1950 is likely to be filled with hair rather than foam, but it's best to be cautious and always use a barrier cloth. Although some natural fibres, such as wool and silk, are inherently flame retardant to some degree, they should still be used with a barrier cloth.

Flameproofing the fabric

Another option is to have your fabric flameproofed by a specialist company, so that it can be used for tight covers without a barrier cloth, or for loose covers. Either send the fabric away for flameproofing, or arrange for someone to come to your home to flameproof the fabric. Bear in mind that the texture and colour of the fabric may be altered slightly by the process. If the fabric has a built-in stain repellent, the chemicals used may not be compatible with those used for flameproofing, so a sample test is advisable to check that there isn't a chemical reaction.

Loose covers

Making your own loose covers is one of the most practical ways of using your sewing skills. You can give an old sofa a new look, or prolong the life of a new chair by making a protective cover.

Sofas and armchairs are often one of the biggest and most costly purchases to make for the home, so you can't afford to replace them too frequently. Making new loose covers is the perfect way to create a completely fresh look for the room, which won't break the budget. Or if you have brand new furniture, you can make covers to protect the furniture from everyday rough and tumble, so that the original tight cover remains pristine for special occasions.

Although it may look complicated, making loose covers is really quite simple. If you already have an old loose cover, you can use this as a pattern for the main cover; otherwise, cut a pattern to fit the sofa in old sheeting or an inexpensive fabric like calico. Insert a zip at one of the back corners of the cover, so that it is easy to remove.

▲ *A new loose cover instantly spruces up a comfortable but unattractive sofa and, since it is removable and washable, it is a practical option for family rooms.*

Use a firmly woven, washable fabric, and take care to match patterns. The pattern should run vertically where possible, and from back to front on the seat.

Making loose covers

These instructions are for a square or box shaped sofa with a straight skirt. To cover a chair or sofa with scrolled or rounded arms, or for a pleated skirt, see overleaf. To avoid costly mistakes a pattern is cut first from old sheeting or calico. Also, to allow for movement, a tuck-in allowance of 15cm (6in) is added along the inside edges of the inner seat panels. You will need a zip about 2.5cm (1in) shorter than the measured height of the sofa back.

The amount of fabric you need depends on the size of the chair or sofa. On average, an armchair takes 5.5-7m (6-7½yd), a two-seater sofa requires 7-9m (7½-10yd), and a three-seater sofa takes about 10-13m (11-14½yd).

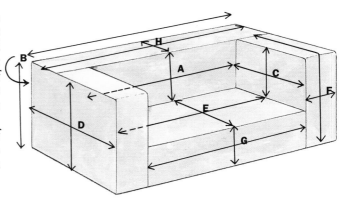

You will need

- ◆ **Furnishing fabrics**
- ◆ **Calico or old sheeting**
- ◆ **Matching sewing thread**
- ◆ **Zip fastener**
- ◆ **Tailors' chalk**
- ◆ **Pins**
- ◆ **Measuring tape**

1 Measuring up Remove any cushions and existing loose covers from the sofa. Measure each panel of the sofa at its widest point and note the measurements, labelling the panels as shown above. Add 5cm (2in) to each measurement to allow for 2.5cm (1in) wide seam allowances on each edge. Add an extra 2.5cm (1in) for hem allowances where necessary. Add 15cm (6in) tuck-in allowances along the lower edges of the inside back (**A**), inside arm (**C**) and the side and back edges of seat (**E**).

2 Cutting out the pattern Cut a rectangle of calico for each sofa panel to the correct sizes, cutting just one set of arm panels. For easy recognition, label the pieces of calico exactly as given in step **1**.

3 Placing the back pieces Position panels **A** and **B** on the sofa, with the tuck-in allowance for **A** positioned along the lower edge. Pin to sofa at the middle of each panel, then smooth out and pin along the edges. Pin the gusset **H** to the top edges of **A** and **B**.

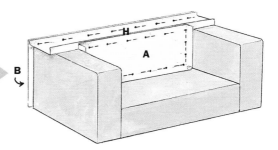

4 Placing the arm pieces Position **D** on the side of the sofa, pinning the back edge to the side edge of **B**. Position **C** with the tuck-in allowance positioned at the lower edge and pin its back edge to the side edge of **A**. Pin the arm gusset **F** to the edges of **C**, **D**, and **H**.

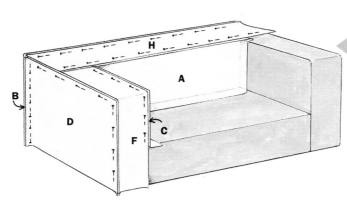

5 Positioning the seat and front pieces Pin the seat piece **E** to the lower edges of **A** and **C**, matching the tuck-in allowances at the back and sides. Then pin the front piece **G** to the front edge of **E** and the lower side edge of **F**. Finally, use tailor's chalk to mark the seamlines around the edge of the sofa on each pattern piece, adding the tuck-in allowances where necessary.

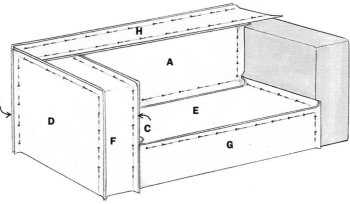

6 **Trimming the pattern pieces** Remove the pieces one at a time, marking them with their name and the pattern or grain direction. Trim the pattern pieces to within 1.5cm (⅝in) of the chalked seamlines, keeping an allowance of 5cm (2in) along all the hem edges.

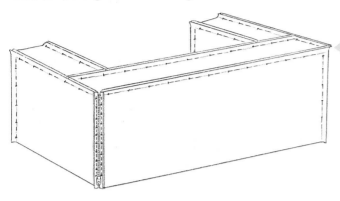

9 **Stitching together** Remove the cover and stitch all the seams in the same order again. Neaten the seam allowances with machine zigzag stitch. On the bottom edge of the cover, press under a double 2.5cm (1in) hem and stitch close to the fold.

10 **Covering the cushions** Measure and make up the covers for the seat cushions following the instructions for box cushion covers on the next page.

▼ *A sofa takes on a completely new look with a brand new loose cover in crisp blue stripes. Here, the cover has been given additional designer flair with simple ribbons made from coordinating gingham fabric.*

7 **Cutting out the fabric** For the large pattern pieces join fabric widths first, adding panels on either side of a central width. Pin the pattern pieces on the fabric, matching the pattern as necessary and following the straight grain. For the arm pieces, cut one set from the pattern, then reverse it for the other side. Cut out all the pieces.

8 **Tacking the cover** With right sides together, pin and tack the cover pieces together, following the same order as before. On one side edge of the outside back panel, pin and tack a zip in place, so that it opens at the bottom edge. Place the tacked cover on the sofa to check the fit; adjust the seams if necessary.

Tip

ADDING PIPING
Piping stitched into the seams gives extra strength – add the piping after checking the fit. Where two seams cross, taper the piping into the seam.

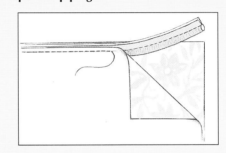

Making a box cushion cover

When re-covering an old box cushion, take the measurements of the existing seat pad, unless it is worn and needs replacing. For a new box cushion, measure the depth and length of the seat to get the size of the foam pad. A box cushion for a recess or a chair with sides should be 6mm (¼in) smaller all round to allow for the thickness of the piping.

To find a foam supplier look in your telephone directory. They can advise on a suitable type and depth of foam – usually from 4cm (1½in) to 7.5cm (3in) thick – and cut it for you from the seat dimensions. With safety in mind, choose flame-resistant, medium-density foam.

You can make the cushions in any size or shape, from a square to a rectangle. You can also button them, with a central button or a balanced arrangement of any number. Position the zip inconspicuously on the back edge of the cushion.

You will need

- ◆ Furnishing fabric
- ◆ Fabric for piping
- ◆ Piping cord
- ◆ Foam pad
- ◆ Zip – 5cm (2in) shorter than one side of the pad
- ◆ Matching thread
- ◆ Tape measure
- ◆ Scissors
- ◆ Pins and a needle
For optional button trim:
- ◆ Self-cover or novelty buttons, 2.5cm (1in) in diameter
- ◆ Waxed button twine
- ◆ Long upholstery needle or darning needle

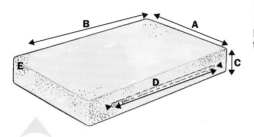

1 Measuring up Measure the width (**A**), the length (**B**) and the depth (**C**) of the pad. To work out the length of the zip (**D**), subtract 5cm (2in) from **B**. Measure all round the sides of the pad and deduct **D** to find the length of the main gusset (**E**).

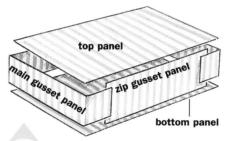

2 Cutting the cushion pieces *For the top and bottom panels*, add 3cm (1¼in) to **A** and **B** and cut two pieces to this size. *For the zip gusset panel*, cut a rectangle **C** plus 6cm (2½in) by the length of the zip **D** plus 3cm (1¼in). *For the main gusset,* add 3cm (1¼in) to **E** and **C** and cut one piece this size.

3 Preparing the piping Buy or make up the piping. You need enough piping to go all round the cushion twice, plus 20cm (8in) for the joins.

4 Attaching the piping Starting at the middle back, apply the piping to the edges of the top piece. At the corners, clip the seam allowance of the piping to the stitching so it lies flat. Join the ends of the piping.

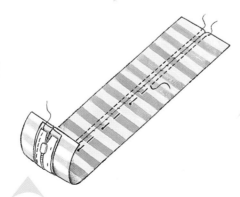

5 Inserting the zip Cut the zip panel in half lengthways, and tack together again with right sides facing, taking a 1.5cm (⅝in) seam allowance. Press the seam open and centre it over the right side of the zip. Pin and stitch down each side, using a zip foot, 6mm (¼in) from the centre seam. Unpick the tacking stitches.

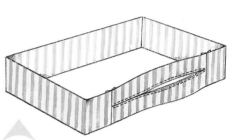

6 Joining the gusset pieces Right sides together, pin and stitch the short ends of the main gusset piece to short ends of zip panel taking 1.5cm (⅝in) seams. This makes a continuous piece. Press seams open.

7 Completing the cushion Staystitch gusset at corner positions. With right sides together, centre zip section of the gusset on back edge of bottom piece. Continue pinning all round, clipping gusset seam allowance at the corners. Stitch. Repeat with the top section, lining up the corners of the top and bottom pieces carefully.

8 Filling the cover Neaten the raw edges with zigzag stitch. Turn to the right side. Roll up the foam pad and insert carefully through the zip, before smoothing out.

Adding a button trim

To give a gusset cushion a neat finish, add matching buttons. You can cover the buttons yourself, to match a gusset cut from a contrasting fabric, for example, or look for novelty buttons in bright colours to match the piping.

2 Preparing to button Buy enough buttons to repeat the pattern top and bottom or cover your own with fabric. Thread an upholstery needle with doubled button twine and knot the ends together. Push the needle through the base centre mark and out at the top centre mark, leaving 15cm (6in) of the knotted ends hanging free.

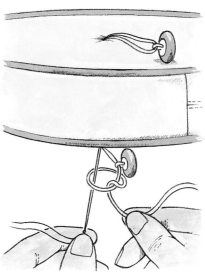

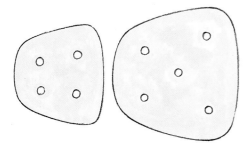

1 Placing the buttons For a centre button, use a tape measure to find the centre point on the top and base of the cushion cover and mark with a dressmaker's pencil. On a rectangular or shaped cushion, space four or five buttons depending on size as in the diagrams above.

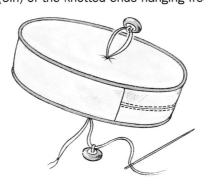

3 Starting to button Thread a button on to the needle end of the twine and pass the needle back through the centre marks on the cushion. Thread another button on to the twine on the other side.

4 Finishing the buttoning Tie the free ends of the twine round the knotted end in a slip knot. Pull the knotted ends of the twine tight so that the buttons sink into the cushion to emphasize its softness. Tie the twine ends off tightly round the button shank and trim.

Covering a rounded chair

The method used for covering a rounded chair is similar to covering a box shaped sofa, but it is even more important to cut the pattern precisely, so that it fits all the curves smoothly.

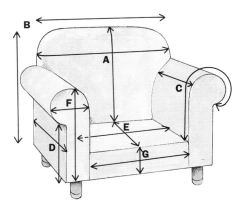

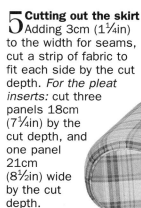

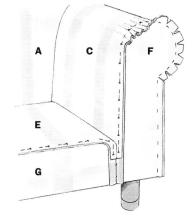

1 Cutting out the pattern Measure the chair and cut out the calico pieces following steps **1-2** on page 12, but omitting the top back gusset **H**. For the arms, cut a separate front panel piece **F**, measuring the widest point of the scroll by the depth of the arm, as shown; then take piece **C** over the arm to meet piece **D** under the scroll.

2 Placing the seat pieces Position pieces **A** and **B** on the chair; pin them together along top of chair back, following any contours. Pin **E** to lower edge of **A**, allowing for the tuck-in. Pin the front gusset **G** to **E**. Pin **C** to **A** and **E**, allowing for tuck-ins at bottom edge; pin **D** to **C** and **B** so seam lies under the arm scroll. Pin **F** in place and draw around shaped outline.

3 Tacking the cover Chalk in the seamlines, trim the pattern and cut out the cover as in steps **5-7** on pages 12–13. Pin and tack cover together, gathering or pleating the fabric around the front of the scroll arm if necessary. Check the fit, then stitch the cover in same order as the tacking. Clip into seam allowances round curves; zigzag to neaten.

4 Measuring for the skirt Fit the cover on the chair. Mark the desired height of the skirt with chalk. For the cut depth, measure from the mark to the floor and add 3.5cm (1½in) for the hem and seam allowances. Measure the width of each side, at the marked height.

5 Cutting out the skirt Adding 3cm (1¼in) to the width for seams, cut a strip of fabric to fit each side by the cut depth. *For the pleat inserts:* cut three panels 18cm (7¼in) by the cut depth, and one panel 21cm (8½in) wide by the cut depth.

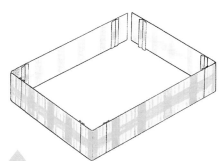

6 Making the skirt Cut the wider panel in half – these pieces fit either side of the zip. Beginning and ending with a half insert, join the skirt strips and inserts right sides together to make one long strip, with a pleat insert between each of the skirt panels. Then neaten the seam allowances.

7 Attaching the skirt Stitch a double 1cm (⅜in) hem on the sides and base of the skirt. Bring seamlines together to pleat up the inserts; pin and tack flattened pleats. With right sides together, pin the skirt to the lower edge of the loose cover, with the half inserts positioned at the bottom of the zip. Tack and stitch. Neaten the skirt seam allowances. Stitch two sets of hooks and eyes to fasten skirt pleat edges together.

Simple chair cover

Revitalize a tired old chair with a top-to-toe cover that simply ties or buttons in place. Made from a single, lined fabric piece, it's quick to sew and fun to trim with details of your choice.

This lined chair cover is cut out in one piece, so it's very quick to put together. The sides meet edge to edge and fasten attractively with neat cord loops and buttons or toggles. Or, for a more casual approach, you can secure them with fabric ties loosely knotted together. If you wish, you can also give the cover a smart, crisp finish by stitching piping round the edge.

Either choose a lining to tone with the main fabric, or go for a contrasting shade, which will add a splash of colour where it peeps out at the cover's joining edges. The cover is fully reversible, so be sure to choose a lining that tones with the surrounding decor for maximum flexibility; you can then simply flip the cover lining-side out when you fancy a change of scene or, on a more practical note, if the main fabric becomes stained.

▲ *Slip-over fabric covers soften the contours of upright dining chairs, giving them a comfortable, welcoming air. They're also an ideal way to help an existing chair blend into a fresh decorative scheme. A tie-on cover, like the one above left, is one of the easiest styles to make.*

Making a button-on chair cover

Choose a firm, closely woven fabric for the cover. On most chairs, 137cm (54in) wide fabric is wide enough to enable you to cut the whole cover in one piece. If using a stripe, you may prefer to cut the side panels separately in order to keep the stripes running vertically all round.

To work out how much fabric to buy, measure from the floor at the back of the chair, up over the chairback, across the seat and down to the floor at the front. Add 10cm (4in) for turnings. Buy this amount of main fabric and lining. You need to buy extra fabric if you want to pipe the cover – see page 20 for instructions on how to do this.

▼ *Black cord fastening loops around natural wood toggles accentuate the colouring of the main fabric in this button-on chair cover.*

You will need

- ◆ **Fabric for cover** – about 2.5m (2³⁄₄yd) of 137cm (54in) wide fabric
- ◆ **Fabric for lining** – same amount as above
- ◆ **Cord for loops** – about 80cm (⁷⁄₈yd)
- ◆ **8 buttons or toggles**
- ◆ **Large sheets of paper**
- ◆ **Masking tape, pencil**
- ◆ **Dressmaker's pencil or tailor's chalk**
- ◆ **Scissors, pins, thread**
- ◆ **Knitting needle**

1 Making the pattern Make one long panel of paper to go over the chair from the floor at the back, up over the chair back (meeting at the sides), and down over the seat to the floor. Tape two pieces to the edges of the seat section for the sides, and cut to fit. Temporarily tape the side edges together to check the fit.

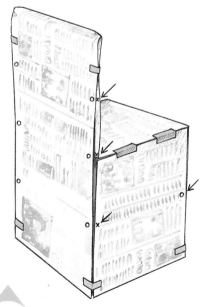

2 Planning the fastenings Mark the fastening positions on each edge of the pattern – one at the junction of the back and seat, one halfway up the back, and one halfway down each leg (see arrows). Mark the button or toggle positions with circles and the loop positions with crosses.

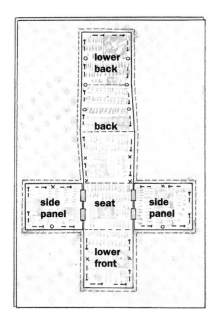

3 Cutting out Lay the fabrics out flat, right sides together. Pin the pattern on top, and mark a 1.5cm (⅝in) seam allowance all round. Cut along the marked line, and transfer the fastening markings to both pieces.

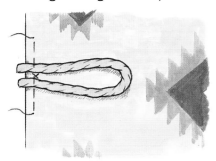

4 Making loops Cut eight 10cm (4in) lengths of cord. Fold each one in half and position it on the right side of the main fabric at a loop position, with the loops facing inwards. Check the loops are big enough for the buttons or toggles, then tack them in place.

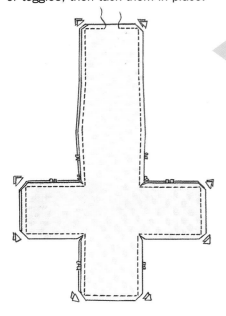

5 Adding the lining Lay the lining and main fabric pieces right sides together and pin all round, matching the fastening marks. Stitch, leaving a 20cm (8in) gap at the centre back. Trim the seam allowances at the outer corners, and clip to just before the stitching line at the inner corners.

6 Finishing off Turn the cover to the right side, pushing the corners out with a knitting needle where necessary, and press. At the opening, turn in the seam allowance and slipstitch closed. Sew buttons or toggles 6mm (¼in) in from the edge opposite the loops, as marked. Place the cover on the chair and slip the cord loops round the buttons or toggles.

▲ *Simple knotted ties add a neat, functional finish to this chair cover. They give you the chance to introduce contrasting fabrics, creating interesting fabric mixes.*

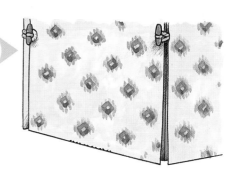

Adding piping

A piped edge gives the chair cover a crisp, tailored finish. Either make your own piping, or buy a slim flanged cord.

You will need

- ◆ **50cm (⅝yd) fabric**
- ◆ **Piping foot**
- ◆ **Piping cord or flanged cord to go all round the cover plus 10cm (4in)**

1 Starting the cover Follow steps **1-3** of *Making a button-on chair cover* on pages 18–19. Make up sufficient piping to go all round the cover plus 10cm (4in).

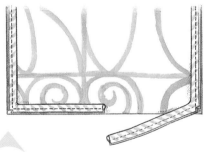

2 Adding the piping Starting on the right side at the centre back of the cover and matching raw edges, pin the piping round the edge, clipping the seam allowance at corners and curves. Stitch the piping in place, joining the ends.

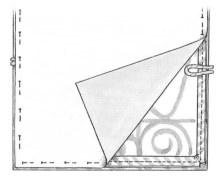

3 Completing the cover To finish, follow steps **4-6** on page 19, laying the cord loops over the piping before you pin and stitch the lining in place. Turn through, then secure the opening by topstitching along the piping stitchline.

Making knotted ties

As a pretty alternative to the tailored button and loop fastenings, make neat knotted ties in a contrasting fabric. You need 0.25m (⅜yd) of fabric for the ties – eight in total. Make up the cover with or without piping as desired.

1 Starting the cover Follow steps **1-3** of *Making a button-on chair cover* on pages 18–19, marking the positions of the fastenings in the usual way. Add piping all round if desired, following *Adding piping*, left.

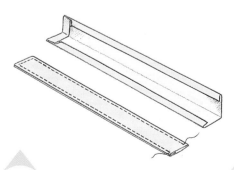

2 Cutting the ties Cut 16 strips of fabric, 22cm (8¾in) long x 7cm (2¾in) wide. On each strip, press in 1cm (⅜in) on both long edges and one short edge. Wrong sides together, fold the strip in half down the length, and stitch round all three turned-in sides close to the edge.

▲ *Detail is all-important on a simple shape. Here the fine stripes of ticking are used for piping on this tie-on cover, giving it a sharp edge and introducing a crisp geometric design to complement the main fabric.*

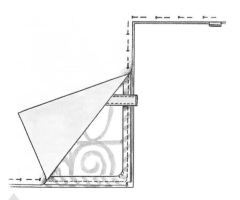

3 Positioning the ties Matching the raw edges, pin a tie across the seamline at each marked point. Follow steps **5-6** on page 19 to complete the cover. Place the cover on the chair and secure the sides by tying each pair of ties into neat reef knots.

Pretty chair covers

A closely fitted, floor-length chair cover effectively softens the outline of all sorts of chairs, unifying your colour scheme and giving the room a fresh, well-dressed look.

Practical and versatile, chair covers are a good way of injecting new life into a room. You can coordinate a set of dining chairs with matching or contrasting fabrics, or dress up a chair for a pretty bedroom. You can even add a soft touch to a bathroom chair with a cosy terry towelling cover.

The cover hugs the back and seat of the chair closely for a snug fit, so that it stays in place. The skirt falls smoothly to the floor with crisp inverted pleats at each corner. The back has another pleat, which is simply caught together with a hook and eye, concealed behind a bow – so you can remove the cover and put it back on without a struggle.

Add your own individual touches of colour and detail to the cover: a fine line of contrasting piping around the seat edge, or soft gathers at the back. The instructions given overleaf are for a crisply tailored bow, but you could make tiny rouleaux bows, or big butterfly bows with long flowing tails instead. Add tassels for a grand, formal touch, neat covered buttons for a smart finish, or tiny pompons for fun. If your chair sits on thick carpet, shorten the skirt slightly to compensate for the pile.

Choose closely woven, washable cotton or linen fabrics which will hold the shape well; woven checks and stripes, floral prints or crunchy natural textures all look effective.

◄ *Smartly tailored pleats give a crisp outline to a pretty floral chair cover; a removable cover is a practical choice for a frequently used chair.*

Making the cover

Check that your chair is a suitable shape for this style of cover. It should have a square-shaped back with a straight top bar, and legs which are not splayed out, as this affects the line of the corner pleats.

Time spent in making a pattern is well worthwhile, as this ensures a neatly tailored fit. If possible, make the pattern before buying your fabric; you can then work out the most economical way of cutting the cover, to avoid wastage. Buy enough piping cord to go round the edge of the seat, finishing at the back edge.

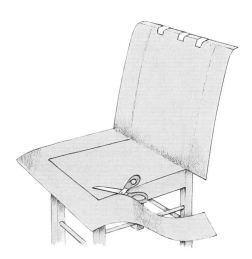

1 Shaping the seat Use masking tape to secure a large sheet of paper to back edge of the top bar. Smooth the paper down the front of the chair back, creasing at junction with the seat. Draw a line round the edge of the seat; cut out along line.

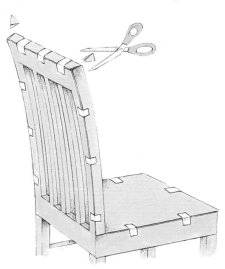

2 Shaping the sides Fold remaining flaps round sides of chair back. Trim down the back edge of the side bars and straight across the bottom edge. At top corners, trim paper level so the edges just meet. Tape in place.

You will need

◆ **Furnishing fabric**

◆ **Contrasting fabric for piping**

◆ **Piping cord**

◆ **Matching thread**

◆ **Large hook and eye**

◆ **Paper and masking tape for pattern**

◆ **Tape measure**

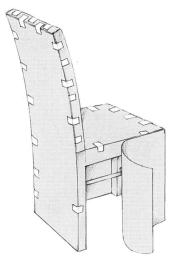

3 Cutting back and skirt patterns *For the back:* tape another piece of paper to back edge of top bar, level with front pattern edge. Trim sides to meet front pattern and trim bottom at floor level. *For the skirt:* tape a sheet of paper all round edge of seat, with top edge meeting edge of seat pattern and side edges level with back panel. Mark seat corners at top edge; trim bottom at floor level.

4 Adding pleats *For the skirt:* cut through the skirt pattern at each corner from the top edge to bottom. Add in a panel of paper 15cm (6in) wide at each corner and side edge. *For the back:* cut down centre of back pattern from top to bottom; add a panel of paper 15cm (6in) wide down the centre, as for the skirt.

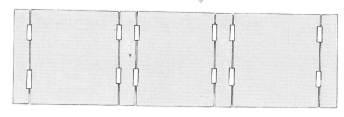

5 Cutting the fabric *For the cover:* lay the pattern pieces on the fabric, allowing seam allowances of 3cm (1¼in) on all hem edges and 1.5cm (⅝in) on all other edges. Cut out, marking in the pleat sections on the skirt and back at the top and bottom edges. *For the bow:* from the fabric, cut a 30cm (12in) square for the bow and a 10 x 7.5cm (4 x 3in) strip for the knot.

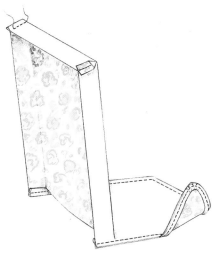

6 Preparing front section Make up and apply piping all round the seat edge. *To form the side gussets:* bring short edges at top corners right sides together; pin and stitch, leaving last 1.5cm (⅝in) open. Press seams open.

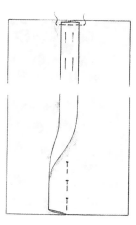

7 Making the back pleat Fold the back piece down the centre, pinning it together at the marked points on top and bottom edges. Flatten pleat, with centre fold on marks. Tack across top and secure with large cross stitches at intervals down the pleat.

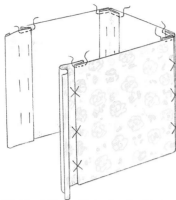

8 **Making the skirt pleats** Make and tack front corner pleats as in step **7**. On back corner pleats, pin and tack in the half of the pleat facing towards front of seat only, leaving back half free.

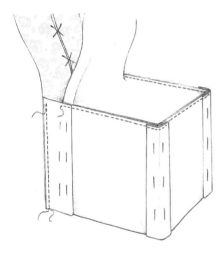

9 **Attaching the skirt** Right sides together and matching centre of front pleats to front corners, pin top edge of skirt to piped edge of front section. Stitch, starting and stopping at centre of back pleats. Then, right sides together and lower edges level, pin side seams of skirt to side edges of lower back piece only. Stitch, stopping 1.5cm (⁵⁄₈in) from top edge of skirt.

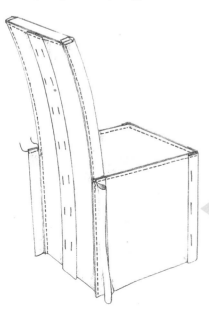

10 **Joining upper back** Right sides together, pin upper back section to upper front section at top and side edges. Stitch, beginning and ending at the stitching line of the piped edge and pivoting at the top corners. Pin and tack remaining half of back pleats.

▲ *Add natty little bows for an amusing detail on a business-like checked cover. The bows shown here are scaled-down versions of the bow for the back: simply cut out smaller pieces for each section.*

11 Neatening the seams Trim all seam allowances to 1cm (³⁄₈in) and zigzag stitch to neaten. On back corner pleats, continue across the top of the free half of the pleat. Press seat edge seam allowances towards the seat and topstitch across top of pleat through back section to secure.

12 Finishing off the cover Remove all the tacking stitches. Put the cover on the chair, wrong side out, to check the length. Turn up the hem level with the floor. Remove cover. Press hemline, then press under 1cm (³⁄₈in) at raw edge; stitch close to the fold.

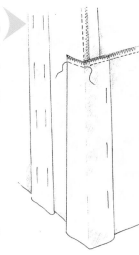

13 Making the bow Work two rows of gathering stitches across the centre of a hemmed rectangle, pull and secure. Wrap the knot strip around to cover the gathers. Stitch, working a few stitches into the back of the bow.

14 Attaching the bow Position the bow centrally over the back pleat, approximately 15cm (6in) above the seat line. Handstitch it in place on one side of the pleat: stitch the hook to the back of the bow on the free side, and stitch the eye to the pleat beneath. Fit the cover on the chair and secure the bow in place.

Optional gathers

On a floral fabric, pretty gathers at the back of the cover make a feminine alternative to a crisp inverted pleat.

1 Starting to make the cover Make pattern as for cover with inverted pleat, steps **1-4** on page 22. Then cut out and begin making up the cover as before, following steps **5-6**.

2 Gathering the back section Divide and mark the top edge of the back piece into three, ignoring the pleat marks. Run a double row of gathering threads between the new central marks, then continue making up the chair cover following steps **8-9**.

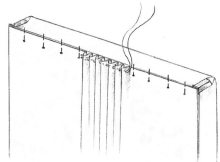

3 Joining upper back sections With right sides together and matching corners, pin back and front sections together at top edge, working from corners inwards as far as gathered section. Pull up gathering threads to fit and pin in place. Omitting reference to pleats, continue making up cover following steps **10-14**, positioning bow to hold gathers loosely.

◄ *An oversized butterfly bow makes an unashamedly romantic statement in a floral scheme.*

Covering a director's chair

*Rejuvenate a basic director's chair with a smart loose
cover – it's an ideal way to give a casual piece of furniture
a more sophisticated look and upholstered feel.*

For both indoor and outdoor use, canvas director's chairs are an inexpensive and versatile form of seating. However, with time, the canvas can become worn and faded and the wooden frame marked.

A simple-to-make loose cover instantly disguises such wear and tear, without restricting the stowable nature of the chair. When the chair is stored away, you can either fold the cover up with it or slip it off so that it does not get too creased. A cover also makes the chair more comfortable by increasing the support around the seat. For additional comfort, you could make a matching cushion or even stitch one in place on the back of the chair.

Choose a fabric to suit the setting for the chairs. For everyday use, make the covers in a mediumweight, washable furnishing fabric – a sturdy cotton is

▲ *Give an old, tired director's chair a
new lease of life by making a smart, new
loose cover for it.*

ideal and easy to stitch. To provide a more opulent, cost-effective seating in a dining room, opt for a lavish, dressy fabric, such as brocade or velvet, and add tassel or cord trims. For a child's bedroom, an animal or theme print cotton is a good option.

Measuring up and cutting a pattern

The chair cover illustrated here is made up in one fabric. For variety and economy you could cut panels from different fabric remnants, but first make sure that the fabrics have similar washing requirements. Measure the chair and make up pattern templates for the cover using pattern paper, tissue or brown paper. Use the pattern pieces to work out the exact fabric requirements for your chair. As a guide, one cover uses approximately 2.5m (2¾yd) of fabric.

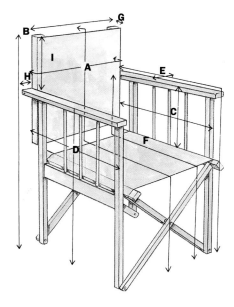

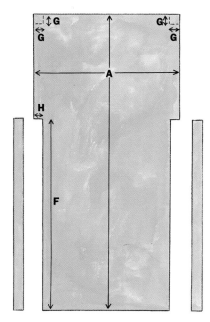

1 Measuring the chair Measure each panel of the chair across its widest points and note down the measurements. From the pattern paper, cut two rectangles to the measurements each of panels (**A**) and (**B**). Cut two rectangles each for panels (**C**), (**D**) and (**E**). Note down the measurements of (**F**), (**G**), (**H**) and (**I**).

2 Trimming the front pattern Mark and cut away a narrow vertical strip measuring **F** by **H** from both lower side edges of panel **A**. At both top corners of panel **A**, measure and mark a square measuring **G** by **G** for the seamlines of the gusset darts.

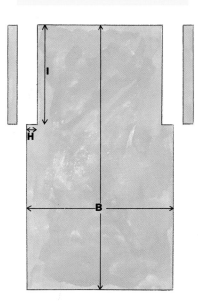

3 Trimming the back pattern To shape the back panel round the arms, mark and cut away a narrow vertical strip measuring **H** by **I**, from both of the upper side edges of panel **B**.

4 Cutting the fabric Following the grain, matching the patterns and centring main design motifs, arrange and pin the pattern pieces on the wrong side of the fabric. Allow a 1.5cm (⅝in) seam and hem allowance all round each piece. Using tailors' chalk, draw round the pattern pieces to mark seamlines. Cut out fabric, including all seam and hem allowances.

◀ *For a really sumptuous effect, use two coordinating fabrics in rich, jewel colours to cover a pair of director's chairs and matching cushion covers.*

A splashy floral is the perfect choice to cover a chair that's destined to live in a conservatory or on a patio, creating a harmonious note with its surroundings.

Making the loose cover

Before making up the panels, reinforce all the corners, where the stitched seam allowances will need to be clipped, with machine stitching. This will prevent the fabric tearing at these points.

1 Assembling the arms Assemble arm panels one at a time. Wrong side up and matching raw edges, pin outside edge of panel **E** around top and front edge of **D**. Ensuring that the corners of the arm rest are level, pin front and top edge of **C** to inside edge of **E**. Clip into seam allowance and across the corners.

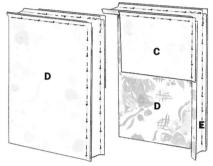

2 Stitching darts in front panel With the right sides together, match the right angled dart seamlines **G** at the top corners of panel **A**. Pin, then stitch the darts. Trim away the excess fabric from the raw edges to the point of each dart.

▼ *If you have two director's chairs in the same room, consider using a different colour-related fabric for each one. For extra comfort, make a matching bolster cushion from a fabric remnant.*

3 Assembling the seat Working from the lower edges upwards and matching the raw edges, pin the inside edges of the arm sections (**C** and lower part of **E**) to either side of panel **A**. Fit the top edge of each arm gusset **E** into the corner extensions of **A**, so that the short edge of **E** is level with the side edge of **A**. Clip into the seam allowances for ease.

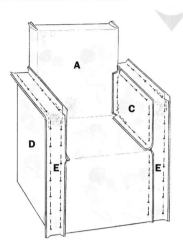

4 Assembling the back Matching the top corners of **B** to the darts in **A**, and with the lower edges even, pin panel **B** to the back edges of the assembled **A**, **D** and **E** section.

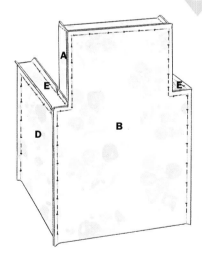

5 Stitching the cover Remove the cover from the chair and, following the pinning sequence, machine stitch the panels together along the marked seamlines. Press the seams, then turn the cover to the right side.

6 Hemming the cover Place the cover over the chair and pin up a narrow double hem all round the lower edge. Remove the cover and neaten all seams with zigzag stitch. Hand or machine stitch the hem and press.

Slip-on footstool cover

A slip-on cover with neatly pleated handkerchief corners and buttoned tabs gives new style appeal to an old footstool. It's quick to stitch and you can simply slip it off for cleaning.

A slip-on cover is a smart and practical way to re-style an old footstool that's past its best, or simply needs updating to suit a new scheme. You can run one up in a fraction of the time it takes to re-upholster, and it has the added advantage of being removable for cleaning when required.

The slip-on cover shown here has a smart, tailored appearance and is pleasingly simple to make. It consists of a lined rectangle of fabric, pleated in at

the corners to fit the stool snugly. The pleats are held with distinctive buttoned tabs. It's a design you can adapt to make other soft furnishing items – a cover for a hall or bedside table, for example, or even a bedcover.

Make the cover from reasonably firm fabrics so that it is hardwearing and holds its shape well – furnishing weight cottons, brocades and velvets are all suitable. The contrast lining shows at the corners, so bear this in mind when

▲ *On this style of slip-on cover, the corner pleats cascade down to the floor, while the sides stop part-way down, allowing the footstool's attractive legs to remain on show.*

making your choice. Here the lining fabric is also used for the corner tabs, with scraps of the main fabric used to cover the buttons; if you prefer, you can introduce one or two new fabrics for these details.

Making the footstool cover

The cover shown here is made to fit a stool 46 x 30 x 30cm (18 x 12 x 12in). The skirt is 18cm (7in) deep, dipping to 26cm (10¼in) at the corner points.

When measuring up for your cover, remember that the corner points will hang down further than the rest of the skirt, so be careful not to make the skirt too long. If in doubt, you can experiment by laying a rectangle of fabric over the footstool and adjusting it to the desired skirt length on two adjacent sides. Check that the corner point stops short of the floor.

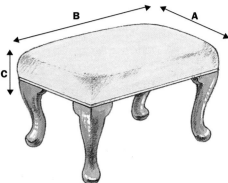

1 Measuring and cutting Measure the width (**A**) and the length (**B**) of the footstool. Decide on the depth of the skirt (**C**). Cut one piece of top fabric **A** plus twice **C** by **B** plus twice **C**, adding a 1.5cm (⅝in) seam allowance all round. Lay it over the footstool to check the effect. Cut a piece of contrast fabric the same size. For the tabs, cut four 18 x 12cm (7 x 4¾in) pieces from contrast fabric.

3 Shaping the tabs Fold each tab in half lengthways, with right sides together. Stitch the long raw edges, taking a 1cm (⅜in) seam and leaving a central 7.5cm (3in) gap. Centre the seam and press open. Place eggcup upside down with its edge 1cm (⅜in) in from one end of a tab. Draw round it from one side of the cup to the other. Repeat at other end of tab. Repeat for each tab.

5 Pleating in the corners Position the cover centrally on the footstool. Mark the centre of each corner by pinching the fabric together and pinning along the diagonal fold. Then pleat in the corners evenly and pin in place.

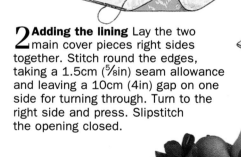

2 Adding the lining Lay the two main cover pieces right sides together. Stitch round the edges, taking a 1.5cm (⅝in) seam allowance and leaving a 10cm (4in) gap on one side for turning through. Turn to the right side and press. Slipstitch the opening closed.

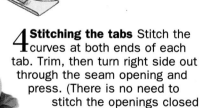

4 Stitching the tabs Stitch the curves at both ends of each tab. Trim, then turn right side out through the seam opening and press. (There is no need to stitch the openings closed – they won't show once the tabs are in place.)

6 Adding the tabs Follow the manufacturer's instructions to cover the buttons with scraps of top fabric. Pin a tab across each corner, halfway down. Remove the cover and stitch a button to each end of each tab, stitching through all fabric layers to secure the folds. Remove the pins.

Tip

REVERSE IDEA If you use a reversible fabric, there is no need to line it. Simply neaten the edges with bias binding. For speedy results use frogging and toggles instead of buttoned tabs.

◀ *For a luxurious colour mix, choose rich red and gold fabrics to make the footstool cover – the perfect complement for the glowing tones of dark wood.*

Fitted footstool covers

A neatly tailored cover gives a useful footstool a smart new look, and you can add an elegantly shaped hem or deep frill. Made in hardwearing cotton, it will provide a practical, washable cover.

Comfortably upholstered footstools and ottomans come in a wide variety of shapes and sizes, and make a useful addition to many areas in a house. The curvy shape of a round footstool has a cosy, welcoming look, while a low ottoman is a popular alternative to a coffee table in the sitting room. A long, narrow stool can also be used as a telephone seat in the hall.

Check secondhand shops, flea markets and auction rooms for old upholstered footstools; you can easily polish up or restain the legs, then add a fresh, washable cover for a magical makeover. You can also buy calico covered stools by mail order.

The instructions are for a cover that is cut to fit the stool closely, so that it looks neat but is easy to slip off for washing. A ruffled frill softens the lower edge of the cover: make it short and sweet, to show off a neatly turned leg below, or longer, to sweep the floor and hide the legs completely. The floor-length cover would work just as well for a round or square pouffe.

For a colourful, fun look, use scraps of different coordinating fabrics for the top, sides, frill and piping. Or opt for a cool, clean look and make the whole cover in one fabric.

◀ *Echo the traditional look of a smart, upholstered armchair by making a slip-over stool cover in a matching checked fabric. Neat piping defines the shape of the cushioned seat pad, while the deep frill, starting at the base of the padded seat and sweeping right down to the floor, covers the legs completely.*

Making the frilled cover

A layer of wadding, fused to the underside of the top section of the cover, gives extra softness, while fusible interfacing adds body to the sides. If you are using a thick upholstery fabric you can omit these layers. Piping defines the top edge – you could add another row at the lower join to balance a longer frill. The frill is cut as a double layer here, as it is only 5cm (2in) deep; a longer frill can be cut as a single layer, with a narrow hem at the bottom.

If you want to wash the cover, make sure that you choose pre-shrunk fabric, or wash the fabric before making up – the close fit of the cover does not allow for shrinkage afterwards.

These instructions are for a round stool, as in the picture, see opposite. For a square or rectangular stool, measure the top of the stool as in step **1** and cut the fabric to these measurements, omitting the paper pattern.

You will need

- ◆ **Furnishing fabric for the top, sides, frill**
- ◆ **Fabric to cover the piping**
- ◆ **Matching thread**
- ◆ **Piping cord**
- ◆ **Fusible wadding**
- ◆ **Mediumweight fusible interfacing**
- ◆ **Paper for pattern, pencil**
- ◆ **Tape measure**
- ◆ **Scissors, pins**

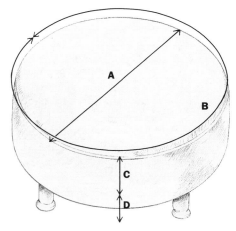

1 Measuring up Measure the diameter of the top (**A**) and the circumference (**B**). Decide on the depth of the side band (**C**) and the depth of the frill (**D**).

2 Making the top pattern Make a circular template to the diameter of the top **A**, adding a 1.5cm (⅝in) seam allowance all round.

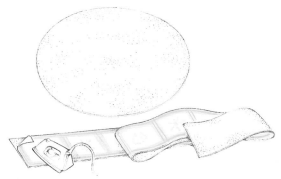

3 Cutting out *For top:* cut one piece each of fabric and fusible wadding from top pattern. Following manufacturer's instructions, fuse the wadding to wrong side of the fabric. *For side band:* add 3cm (1¼in) to both **B** and **C** and cut one piece to this size, centring any motifs. Cut one piece of interfacing to same size, and fuse to wrong side of fabric.

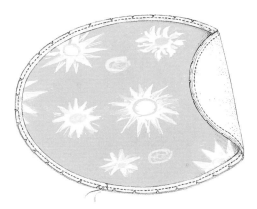

4 Applying the piping Make up enough piping to go all round the edge of the top piece, plus 10cm (4in) for the join. Apply the piping all round the top edge, clipping the seam allowance if necessary and joining the ends neatly.

5 Stitching the side band Right sides together, pin and stitch the short ends of the side band together; trim the seam allowances and press them open.

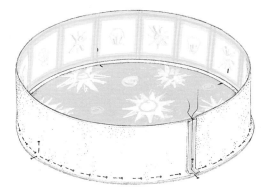

6 Assembling the cover Divide the piped edge of the top piece and the top edge of the side band into quarters, marking each with a pin. With right sides and raw edges together, and matching the marks, pin and stitch the side band to the top piece.

7 Cutting the frill Double the circumference of the stool **B** and add 3cm (1¼in). Then, cutting across the width of the fabric and joining widths as necessary, cut a strip to this measurement by twice **D** plus 3cm (1¼in).

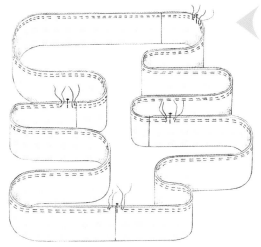

8 Making the frill Join the strips together and make a folded frill, marking the raw edges into quarters and working two rows of gathering threads along the raw edges.

▲ *Here, remnants of four coordinating fabrics have been put to good use — cleverly teamed together to make a charming cover for a small footstool.*

9 Attaching the frill Fold the lower edge of the side piece into quarters and mark the folds with pins. With right sides and raw edges together, pin the frill to the lower edge of the side band, matching pins. Pull up the gathering stitches on the frill evenly to fit. Tack in place, then stitch. Remove tacking stitches and neaten raw edges.

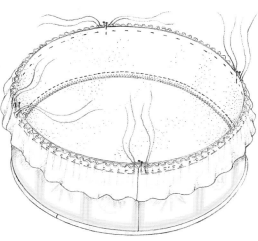

Shaped cover

As a fun alternative, make a jester-style stool cover. The sides are lined with a contrasting fabric, so interfacing is not necessary here, but it is used to give body to the top. If you're nervous about drawing curves, use a Flexible curve as a guide. You could use tassels, pompons or beads in place of bells, if you wish.

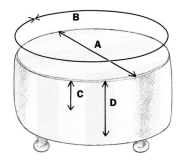

1 **Measuring up** Measure the diameter (**A**) and circumference (**B**) of the stool as in step **1** on page 32. *For the side band:* decide on the shortest depth (at the top of the scallop) (**C**) and the longest depth (at the point) (**D**).

2 **Cutting out the top** Using interfacing instead of wadding, follow steps **2-3** on page 32 to make a pattern and cut out the top piece. Fuse the interfacing to the wrong side of the fabric.

3 **Making the side band** Add 3cm (1¼in) to both **B** and **D** and cut a piece each of fabric and lining to this size. Join the short sides of each side band as in step **5** on page 32, then tack the two bands right sides together along the lower edge. Divide the band into seven equal sections, marking with pins.

4 **Making a template** Cut a piece of card the width and depth of one of the marked fabric sections. Add 3cm (1¼in) to **C** and mark this point at the centre of the template. Using the flexible curve, draw a curve from one bottom corner up to **C** and back down again. Cut out along the curved line.

▲ *Hanging bells add a jolly touch to this footstool cover, while the reverse scallops reveal the stool's toning stripes.*

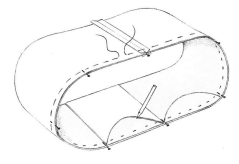

5 **Marking the scallops** On the wrong side of the fabric, use the template to mark in a scallop at the lower edge in each of the seven sections.

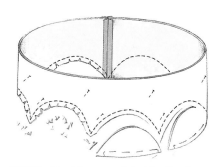

6 **Stitching lower edge** Pin the layers together, then stitch all round the scallops, 1.5cm (⅝in) up from marked line. Trim along marked line, clipping into curves and snipping across the points. Turn right side out and press.

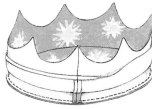

7 **Assembling the cover** Leaving the lining free, follow step **6** on page 32 to join the side band to the top piece. Press the seam allowances towards the top band. Then press under a 1.5cm (⅝in) seam allowance on the top edge of the lining.

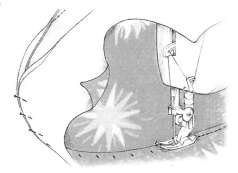

8 **Finishing off** On the inside, bring pressed edge of the lining over the raw edges of the fabric and pin, lining up the folded edge with the stitching line. On the right side, topstitch through all layers 3mm (⅛in) below the first stitching line, making sure you catch in the edge of the lining. Stitch a small bell to each point.

Dressing table cover

*Turn a battered or outdated piece of furniture into a stylish
and functional asset with a crisply cut cover — you can adapt it to
fit furniture of any shape, and make a matching stool cover too.*

It's a shame to get rid of furniture just because it looks old-fashioned, is stained, or doesn't fit in with a new colour scheme. A fabric cover solves the problem easily, hiding blemishes and adding a fresh new look to a room. The practical design of this dressing table cover includes a short flap at the front, enabling you to sit at the table comfortably, and gives easy access to the drawer.

A wide border, with neatly mitred corners, emphasizes the simple lines. The border binds the raw edges of the skirt so that it looks neat from both sides. As the edges of the cover are all straight, there's no need to cut the binding on the bias, but joined ends are cut at an angle so that the seams are less obvious. The top section of the cover is lined with contrasting fabric. The skirt

▲ *Cream calico makes the perfect partner for the spring green and cream of this classical print cover. Covers like this are a good way of coordinating assorted pieces of furniture to suit a new scheme.*

is left unlined, so it is best to make any joins with flat-fell seams. Buttons finish off the corners of the flap, and this detail is repeated on the matching stool cover.

Making the dressing table cover

Decide on the length of the skirt before buying the fabric. You can make it to the floor, but the three-quarter length shown here adds a fresh look and is more convenient. The main skirt stops short on either side of the drawer to allow for easy access. The centre drawer panel is cut 12cm (5in) wider than the drawer so that it overlaps the main skirt.

If you want to protect your cover with a panel of glass, ask your local glazier to cut 6mm (¼in) thick toughened glass to fit the table top.

You will need

◆ **Furnishing fabric**

◆ **Contrasting fabric for the border and lining**

◆ **Two large buttons**

◆ **Matching thread**

◆ **Tape measure**

◆ **Scissors, pins**

▶ *The crisp, square lines of the cover are clearly emphasized with wide borders and outsized buttons. Austere lines like these are typical of the Scandinavian style; substitute a blue and cream check for another classic combination.*

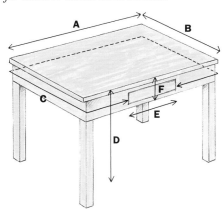

1 Measuring up Measure the width (**A**) and depth (**B**) of the dressing table top. *For the main skirt width:* measure around the table top from one side of the drawer to the other (**C**); decide on the skirt length (**D**). *For the drawer panel:* measure the width (**E**) and depth (**F**) of the drawer.

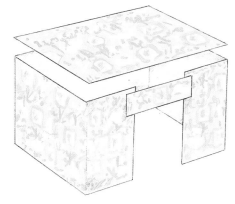

2 Cutting out *For top panel:* add 3cm (1¼in) to **A** and **B** and cut one piece from both fabric and lining. *For main skirt:* add 1.5cm (⅝in) to **D** and cut enough fabric widths to make up **C** when joined. *For drawer panel:* add 12cm (5in) to **E** and 2.5cm (1in) to **F**; cut one piece in fabric to this size.

3 Cutting out the border Measure all round the bottom and side edges of the main skirt piece and drawer panel. Cut enough 10cm (4in) wide strips of contrasting fabric, on the straight of the grain, to go all round both, allowing 50cm (20in) extra for mitres and joins.

Tip

PREVENTING SHADOWS
If the main fabric shows through to the right side of the border, follow the instructions up to step 6, then trim it away to slightly less than the border seam allowances.

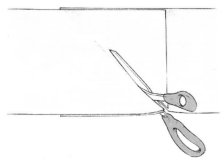

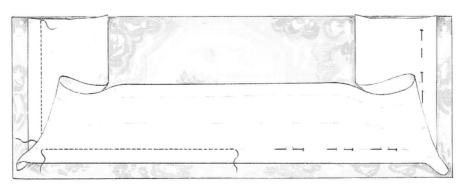

4 Preparing the border strips Use angled seams to reduce bulk: with strips right side up, overlap ends by 10cm (4in). Fold top end level with one side edge, finger press fold, then open it out and cut along fold through both layers. Join as for bias binding. Press seams open, then press under 1.5cm (⅝in) on both long edges of the strip. Fold the strip in half lengthways with folded edges aligned and press.

5 Pinning border to drawer panel Right sides together, position one raw edge of border 2cm (¾in) in from the side edge of the drawer panel. Pin, stopping 3.5cm (1⅜in) from lower panel edge. Leave 4cm (1½in) border free to form the mitred corner, then continue pinning border along lower edge, with raw edge still 2cm (¾in) from lower edge of panel. Repeat at the remaining corner and side.

6 Stitching the border Machine stitch along the foldline of one side border, stopping exactly 3.5cm (1⅜in) from lower panel edge. Backstitch to reinforce the stitching, then trim thread ends. Reposition fabrics to stitch the lower edge, folding 4cm (1½in) excess out of the way and starting the stitching exactly at the point where you stopped. Repeat for remaining corner and side.

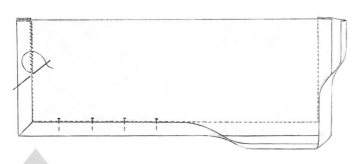

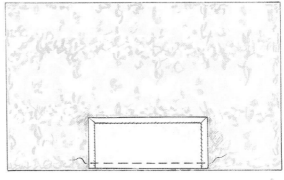

7 Finishing border Turn border to wrong side along its centre fold, folding each corner pleat to one side. On wrong side, pin folded edge level with stitching, making pleats at corners to match those on right side. Slipstitch folded edge to stitching.

8 Making the main skirt Join the panels with flat-fell seams, as necessary, to make up the required width. Following steps **5-7** above and left, add the border to the lower and side edges of the main skirt.

9 Positioning drawer panel With right sides together and raw edges matching, centre the drawer panel on the front edge of the top panel. Pin and tack the drawer panel in place.

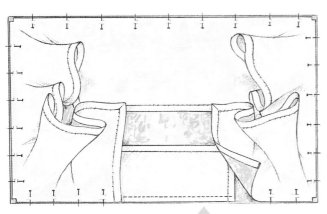

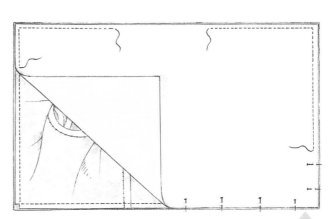

10 Adding the main panel Mark centres of top edge of main skirt and back edge of top panel. Right sides together and matching the centres, pin skirt round edge of top panel, clipping and easing at corners and overlapping ends of drawer panel.

11 Stitching the cover together Stitch round the top panel, stitching through all the layers and pivoting the fabric at the corners. Trim the seam allowances in layers to reduce excess bulk.

12 Lining the top panel With right sides together, pin the top panel lining to the top panel, sandwiching the skirt in-between. Stitch in place, leaving a 20cm (8in) gap. Turn cover through to the right side and slipstitch the opening closed.

Making the stool cover

It's easy to turn a plain wooden, metal or plastic stool into a comfortable seat to match your dressing table. The cover for the stool is made in the same way as for the dressing table, but the skirt is cut in one piece and joined to make a loop.

This cover is designed for a square or rectangular stool with straight legs. For comfort, you can add a foam squab, cut to fit. Make the cover to finish just off the floor, to allow for the hem to drop a little when the foam is compressed.

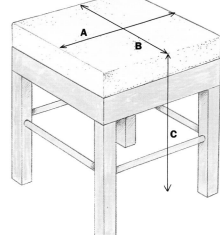

You will need

◆ **Furnishing fabric**

◆ **Contrasting fabric for binding**

◆ **Matching thread**

◆ **Eight large buttons**

◆ **5cm (2in) thick foam squab to size of stool top (optional)**

◆ **PVA adhesive**

▼ *A neat, simple cover turns a bargain stool into an elegant seat. The big buttons add the all-important finishing touch.*

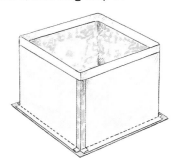

1 Measuring up Glue or secure the foam squab in place on the seat. Measure the top following step **1** of *Making the dressing table cover* on page 36; *for skirt depth*, measure from the top of the foam.

2 Cutting out *For the top panel:* cut a piece of fabric to fit top of foam (**A** by **B**) plus 1.5cm (⅝in) all round. *For the skirt:* cut a rectangle of fabric to go all round edge of top piece (twice **A** plus twice **B**), adding 5cm (2in) for seam allowances and ease, by the skirt depth (**C**) plus 1.5cm (⅝in).

3 Making the border Follow steps **3-4** on previous pages to cut and prepare a border strip the same length as skirt.

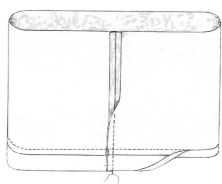

4 Making the skirt Pin and stitch border to base of skirt as in steps **5-6** on the previous page. With border opened out, join short sides of skirt and border to make a loop. Press seam open. Complete border as before, following step **7**.

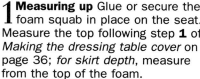

5 Joining skirt to top Right sides and raw edges together, and matching skirt seam to one of the corners, pin and stitch skirt to top panel. Clip into skirt seam allowance to ease it round corners, then trim and neaten seams.

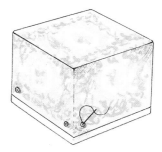

6 Finishing off On each corner, stitch two buttons, positioning each one 2.5cm (1in) above the border and 2.5cm (1in) away from each corner.

Dressing table skirts

*A traditional kidney-shaped dressing table makes a
pretty feature in a feminine bedroom, and a cover with a
flowing skirt accentuates its gently rounded shape.*

Give your bedroom a touch of romance and old-fashioned glamour with a graceful, full-length dressing table cover. You often come across old dressing tables made in a kidney-shaped style in secondhand shops. Don't worry if there are any stains and scuffs on the table top, as these will be completely hidden by the cover. Alternatively, you can buy the dressing table base by mail order or from do-it-yourself and furniture shops, and cover it to coordinate with your bedroom's decor.

The table does not have to be limited to a kidney shape either. If you prefer, you can use any small table with a drawer, as long as it has a lip that extends beyond the base; the lip on the table top is necessary as the dressing table curtains are hung from it.

Traditionally, dressing tables have at least one drawer beneath the table top. The cover includes a skirt which is split at the front and hangs like a curtain on a fixed track under the table edge, so that it can be pulled aside for easy access to the drawer. The top has a deep frill which hides the track – working in a very similar way to a curtain valance. You can use contrasting patterned or plain fabrics for the frill and skirt if you wish, with a fine line of piping round the top to add definition to the shape.

To really play up the feminine look, you can add a frill at the bottom of the skirt and a double frill round the top edge. This gives a wonderfully frivolous, light-hearted feel to your dressing table and to the look of your bedroom.

◄ *A pretty and playful table cover can make all the difference to a little girl's room, especially when matched with coordinating curtains and wallpaper. Here, a novelty nursery print is teamed with smart, gingham checks in complementary colours to produce a stylish bedroom accessory.*

Making the dressing table cover

The cover consists of a lined top cover with an attached frill. The skirt is hung separately from heading tape. Choose a lightweight, flexible top-fixing track, and fix it to the underside of the table top, about 2.5cm (1in) in from the edge. If your table has no drawer, you can simply attach both the skirt and frill on to the top piece. For a professional finish, take a template of the table top to a glazier and get the shape cut in 5mm (¼in) thick glass. Placed on top, this keeps the finished cover firmly in place and protects the fabric from spills.

You will need

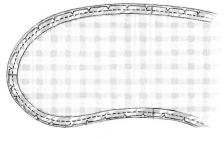

- ◆ Furnishing fabric for the top, skirt and frill
- ◆ Fabric for piping
- ◆ Piping cord
- ◆ Lining fabric
- ◆ Standard curtain heading tape
- ◆ Matching thread
- ◆ Large sheet of paper
- ◆ Dressmaker's pencil

1 Measuring up Measure round the top edge of the dressing table (**A**). Then measure the length from the eye of the track runner to the floor, and add 5.5cm (2⅛in) to allow for the heading and hem (**B**). Finally, decide on the length of the top frill, remembering that it should cover the track and the curtain heading completely, and add 3.5cm (1⅜in) (**C**).

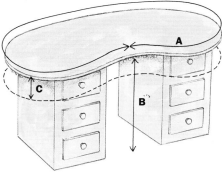

2 Cutting the top Lay a sheet of paper on top of the table and make a crease to mark the edge by pressing round the sides. Cut along the crease. Using this as a pattern, and adding 1.5cm (⅝in) all round, cut one piece from both lining and fabric.

3 Cutting the skirt and frill pieces *For the skirt:* multiply **A** by 1½, and cut enough fabric widths equal to this measurement by the length of **B**. *For the frill:* cut enough fabric widths to measure twice **A** by the length of **C**.

▶ *Create a coordinating bedroom set by making a standard cover for your dressing table, then cover the stool in the same way as the top but make the frill longer and add a gusset the depth of the padded seat.*

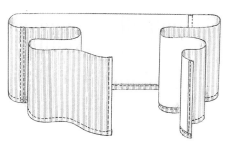

4 Hemming the skirt Using flat fell seams, join the widths to make a long strip. On each short end, press under a 1.5 cm (⅝in) double hem; pin and stitch. Make a hem in the same way on the bottom edge.

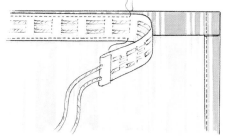

5 Adding heading tape Press under 2.5cm (1in) along the top edge of the skirt. Then, with the top edge of the tape just below the folded edge, pin the heading tape along the skirt top; trim any fabric sticking out below the tape. Finish ends and stitch.

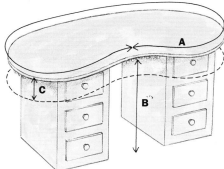

6 Piping the top Cut enough bias strips to the length of **A**, plus 10cm (4in) for the join. Make up the piping and apply all round the edge of the top piece. Then fold the top into quarters and mark the edge at the foldlines.

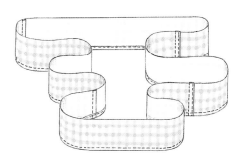

7 Hemming the frill Using flat fell seams, join the frill widths to make a continuous loop. Then press under a double 1cm (⅜in) hem on the lower edge; stitch close to the fold.

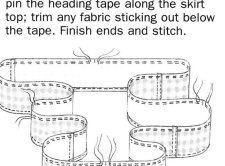

8 Gathering the frill Fold the frill into quarters and mark on the top edge. Stopping and starting at each quarter mark, work two rows of gathering stitches round the top, 1cm (⅜in) then 1.2cm (½in) from the raw edge.

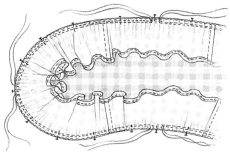

9 Adding the frill With right sides together and matching the marks and raw edges, pin the frill to the edge of the top piece, sandwiching the piping between. Pull up and adjust the gathers to fit, then tack.

10 Lining the top Place the top piece and the lining right sides together, with the frill sandwiched between. Pin and stitch all round, leaving a 10cm (4in) opening at the centre back for turning through. Trim and clip the seam allowances, layering them to reduce bulk. Turn out to the right side through the opening. Press, then slipstitch the opening closed.

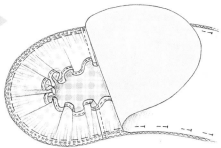

11 Finishing off Pull up the cords of the skirt heading tape to fit the length of the track, and then tie them off. Adjust the fabric gathers evenly, and then insert the hooks and hang the skirt. Place the top piece on the dressing table top, smoothing it down over the skirt. Position the glass so that it fits snugly inside the piping ridge.

Making a box-pleated skirt

For a tailored, elegant look, make this crisply pleated version of the dressing table cover. The skirt is attached to the top instead of hanging separately. You can keep it short and sweet, as shown here, or make it full-length. Alternatively, add a second split, gathered skirt below the pleats for access to drawers. Remember that for box pleats you need three times the finished width.

1 Measuring up Referring to step **1** on page 40, measure round the top of table. Decide on the skirt depth and add 3.5cm (1⅜in) (**C**).

2 Cutting the top Follow step **2** on page 40 to make a pattern for the top; use it to cut one piece each from fabric and lining.

3 Making the skirt Multiply **A** by three. Cut enough fabric widths the length of **C** to make up this measurement when joined together in a continuous loop. Follow steps **6-7** on page 40 to pipe and mark the top, and to join and hem the skirt.

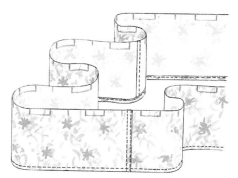

4 Marking the pleats Divide **A** into an equal number of pleats – the ones shown here are 5cm (2in) wide. Starting at the centre back seam, mark the pleats.

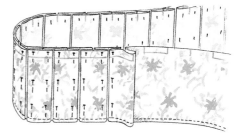

5 Pleating up Make and tack the pleats in place. Check that the final measurement equals **A**.

6 Making up the cover Divide top edge of the skirt into quarters and mark. Follow step **10** on previous page to pin and tack the skirt to the top, add the lining and turn to right side.

▲ *There are all sorts of variations in style for making dressing table covers. This mini box-pleated skirt lends an elegant and smart look, as well as being practical, allowing room for putting your legs under the table if you wish to sit closer to the mirror.*

Sheer lampshade covers

Use crisp, sheer fabrics to make a flirty overskirt
for a lampshade – a quick and effective way
to revamp an old, faded shade.

Lightweight, gauzy fabric, gathered into a full and flouncy skirt, gives a touch of glamour to even the simplest lamp. You can update an old lampshade, or buy an inexpensive, plain one to work on. If the colour of the shade is wrong, choose an opaque fabric like taffeta, light silk or fine cotton. If the colour matches the room, you can show it off very effectively with a sheer skirt that lets the base colour glow

through – try green organza over gold, perhaps, or white spotted net over a rose pink shade.

Make the most of the flirty shape with velvet or taffeta ribbon for a dramatic bow; add a twist of rope to natural muslin, or wired ribbon for sculptural effects. For extra emphasis, trim the lower edge of the skirt with fine ribbon or a dainty trim, or just finish the edge with pinking sheers for a speedy job.

▲ *Delicate white chiffon, gathered up and tied in place on the plainest of white lampshades, makes a dreamy addition to a very feminine dressing table.*

Two methods are given on the following pages. The first is for a covering a shaped (bowed) lampshade with a cover and a separate skirt. The second gives instructions for making a flirty skirt to sit on top of a coolie shade.

Covering shaped lampshades

This idea is an excellent way of covering a bowed or waisted lampshade (one which curves inwards at the centre). The new cover is made in two sections: first a cover that sits over the entire lampshade; then a separate skirt – both held in place with elastic casing. The skirt sits part-way down, on the waist of the lampshade, with the join hidden by a wide ribbon. For the best effect, cut the skirt long enough to overhang the shade by about 1cm (⅜in).

You will need

- ◆ Fabric
- ◆ Matching thread
- ◆ 50mm (2in) wide ribbon
- ◆ Bowed drum or waisted lampshade
- ◆ 6mm (¼in) wide elastic
- ◆ Paper for making a pattern
- ◆ Two safety pins
- ◆ Scissors
- ◆ Tape measure
- ◆ Ruler and pencil
- ◆ Needle and pins

▼ *Shocking pink organza makes a flamboyant statement as a frou-frou lampshade skirt. The splash of yellow contrasts wickedly with the vivid colour of the shade and spotted bow trim. The band and bow are stitched on separately.*

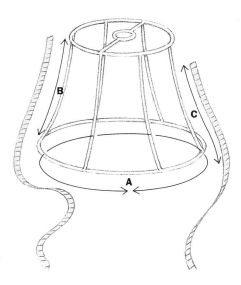

1 Measuring up Use a tape measure to measure round the base of the shade (**A**) and down one side (**B**). Then decide on the skirt depth (**C**).

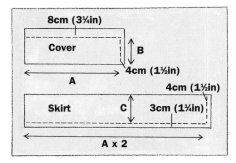

2 Cutting out *For the cover:* On paper draw a rectangle to the dimensions **A** plus 4cm (1½in) by **B** plus 8cm (3¼in). *For the skirt:* draw a rectangle **C** plus 3cm (1¼in) by twice **A** plus 4cm (1½in). Use the paper patterns to cut out one cover and one skirt panel from the fabric.

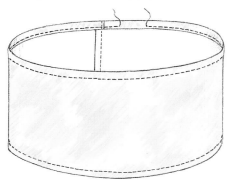

3 Stitching the cover Using a French seam, join the short ends of the lining. To make casings for the elastic, turn up a 3mm (⅛in), then 1.2cm (½in) hem on both long edges. Stitch, leaving 2.5cm (1in) opening in each casing to insert the elastic.

▶ *Add a touch of glamour to a lampshade with a golden lining topped with a starstruck net overskirt and trimmed with a shimmering gold ribbon.*

4 Fitting the lining Thread the elastic through each casing and hold the ends together with safety pins. Put the lining over the shade, pulling up the elastic to fit snugly around the base and top. Take the lining off. Trim the ends of the elastic and stitch together. Slipstitch the casing openings closed, then refit the lining on the shade.

5 Stitching the skirt Using a French seam, join the two short ends of the skirt. Make a casing on one long edge by turning up a 3mm (⅛in), then 1.2cm (½in) hem. Stitch casing, leaving an opening for the elastic.

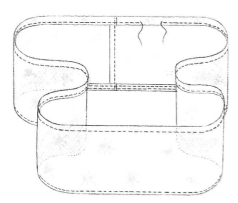

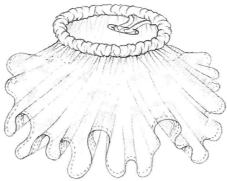

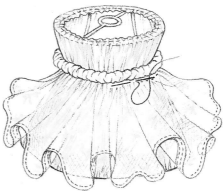

6 Hemming the skirt On remaining long edge, stitch a narrow topstitched hem: press under a 6mm (¼in) hem to the wrong side and stitch close to the fold. Press under a further 6mm (¼in), so that the first row of stitching sits to the wrong side, and then stitch close to new fold.

7 Fitting the skirt Thread the elastic through the casing and secure with a safety pin. Fit the skirt over the shade and pull up the elastic so that the skirt hugs the shade snugly. Remove the skirt. Stitch the ends of the elastic together and slipstitch the casing opening closed.

8 Completing the shade Slip the skirt over the lined shade and fix it in place with a few neat stitches. Tie ribbon or rope round the waist of the skirt to hide the join and fix it in place with a few stitches, if necessary. To finish, trim the top of the skirt with a separate bow, rosette or silk flower.

Coolie shades

You can add a swirly skirt to a conical coolie shade. This skirt is simply glued to the top of a small coolie shade – these are inexpensive and readily available from most lighting and department stores. If you don't already have one that needs re-covering, buy a new one in a toning colour to the fabric you are using. The gathering is set down from the top of the skirt to form a pretty top frill – allow for this when buying your fabric.

You will need

- ◆ Coolie lampshade
- ◆ Fabric
- ◆ Matching sewing thread
- ◆ Ribbon for covering over the gathering line
- ◆ Paper for making a pattern
- ◆ Scissors
- ◆ Tape measure
- ◆ Ruler and pencil
- ◆ Needle and pins
- ◆ All purpose adhesive

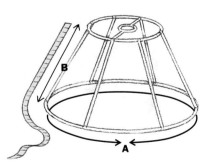

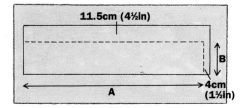

1 Making a paper pattern Measure round the base of the lampshade (**A**) and down the side (**B**). Using a pencil and ruler, draw a rectangle **A** plus 4cm (1½in), by **B** plus 11.5cm (4½in) on to the paper. Cut out the paper pattern.

2 Hemming the skirt Pin the pattern on to the fabric and cut it out. Join the two short ends with a French seam. Hem one long edge as in step **6** on page 45.

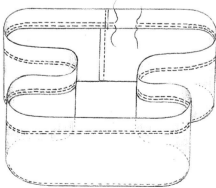

3 Gathering the skirt Turn over 10cm (4in) to wrong side along top edge. Stitch two rows of gathering close to raw edge and 5mm (¼in) away. Place skirt over shade, and draw up gathers to fit around the top. Even out gathers and tie off the threads to secure.

▲ *A haze of white chiffon forms a delicate shade that complements the crystal base to perfection. To make the self tie, cut a rectangle of fabric and neaten the edges with a narrow, topstitched hem.*

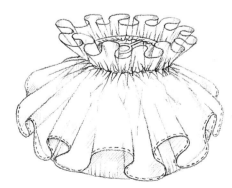

4 Finishing off Place the skirt on the shade, so the frill extends above top of shade. Secure it in place with a few dabs of adhesive around the top of shade. When the adhesive is dry, carefully tie the ribbon around the shade, over the gathering line. Alternatively, make a self tie.

Covered coathangers

A padded coathanger is more than a decorative accessory.
It helps keep a garment in shape while hanging, and prevents the
distortion that can happen on a hard, uncovered hanger.

Ensure that your clothes stay in good condition and looking pristine by storing them on covered coathangers. While shop-bought covered hangers can be expensive, plain wooden hangers are cheap and easy to find in department stores. Use fabric remnants to cover them, to make your own padded hangers inexpensively.

First pad around the coathangers with wadding. The amount of padding you add depends on how much support you need to give the garment. A jacket or coat, for instance, requires a large, well-rounded hanger to keep it in shape, while a silk blouse needs much less padding.

The cover consists of two rectangles of fabric, gathered on to the hanger by hand. Use a lightweight fabric, to make the gathering easier. For a luxurious finishing touch, slip a scented sachet, made in the same fabric as the cover, over the completed hanger.

▼ *Gleaming brocade and crisp taffeta fabrics turn humble wooden hangers into romantic bedroom accessories. Twists of organza ribbon tied around the hooks make them even more covetable.*

Covering a hanger

Wooden hangers are sold in different sizes for children's through to men's clothing, so select a size that is suitable for the garment you plan to support. As you are padding the hanger first, you do not need to use expensive hangers as the base. Supermarkets are a good place to look for well priced hangers and they are often sold in packs.

You will need

- ◆ Wooden coathanger
- ◆ 20cm (¼yd) of 100g (4oz) wadding
- ◆ Fabric remnant, at least 8cm (3¼in) wide by three times the length of hanger
- ◆ Hand sewing needle
- ◆ Thread to match fabric
- ◆ Scissors
- ◆ Pins

▼ *If you have enough fabric, why not make small scented sachets as well? These are made from rectangles of fabric, seamed across the base and side. Tie them in place with a length of narrow ribbon.*

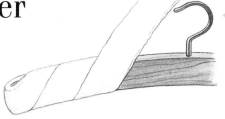

1 Padding the hanger Cut the wadding into 5cm (2in) wide strips. Wrap the wadding horizontally around one end of the hanger, then diagonally around it. Add in new strips as needed. To finish, wrap wadding around remaining end of coathanger and secure with a few hand stitches. Repeat, for a more padded effect.

2 Cutting out the cover Measure the length of the padded hanger (**A**) and the circumference (**B**). Cut two strips of fabric at least 1½ times **A** by half **B** plus 3cm (1¼ in).

3 Preparing the cover Place the fabric strips right sides together and stitch down both short ends. Press the seams open, then press 1cm (⅜in) to the wrong side along each long edge. Turn to right side.

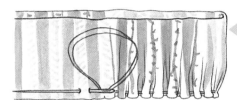

4 Gathering up the cover Using doubled thread, work a row of running stitches about 3mm (⅛in) long, close to the folded edges of one side, keeping folds aligned. Slip cover on to the hanger and pull up, gathering to fit. Fasten off thread.

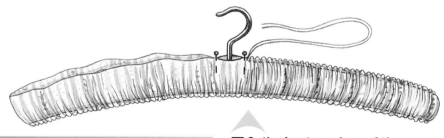

5 Gathering top edges of the cover Using pins, secure the cover to the wadding on both sides of the metal hook. Using double thread and starting at one end, work running stitches along the folded edges up to the hook. Pull up the gathering to fit and secure thread ends. Repeat to stitch the remaining edge.

Tip

PADDING
Old tights or stockings make excellent padding and can be used in place of wadding. Wash the hosiery first, and use just the leg section of tights. Wrap the tights firmly around the hanger, adding in more tights until you have the desired amount of padding.

Fabric-covered boxes

*Store treasured keepsakes or odds and ends in an
attractive stack of fabric-covered boxes – they are simple
to make without even sewing a stitch.*

Old cardboard boxes provide valuable extra storage space, but their unsightly looks mean they are usually designated to hidden corners of a room. Cover them in fabric to match your decor and you'll be happy to put them on display, with the added advantage that the contents will be more readily accessible. For instance, a box covered in pretty fabric and filled with jewellery makes a tasteful addition to a dressing table. A stack in a corner of your bedroom can house a collection of shoes or hats, and living room shelving can be kept clutter-free if boxes are used to store CDs, cassette tapes and other paraphernalia.

You can use any sturdy cardboard box with a lid – shoe and hat boxes are both ideal, or try stationery and craft shops, who sometimes supply plain card boxes. When it comes to covering the box, choose a fabric in colours and patterns to tie in with the style of the room.

▲ *Stacks of boxes of various shapes and sizes, covered in beautiful furnishing fabrics are a visual treat. It is also a great way of displaying remnants of fabric you can't bear to throw away.*

Most fabrics are suitable, but avoid fine or slippery fabrics and heavy fabrics, such as a textured tweed. Firmly woven, mediumweight fabrics, such as chintz and furnishing cotton, are ideal.

Covering a square or oblong box

You will need

- ◆ **Box with lid**
- ◆ **Fabric**
- ◆ **Spray adhesive**
- ◆ **Fabric glue or general purpose adhesive**
- ◆ **Tape measure**
- ◆ **Scissors**
- ◆ **Pencil**

◀ *Why not cover the box lid with a different, coordinating fabric if you don't have enough for the whole box? Or, use exactly the same technique to cover a box with remnants of wallpaper.*

Materials

Use a light adhesive, such as spray adhesive, to avoid seepage through the fabric. Secure the turnings and edges with a fabric glue or general purpose adhesive. As a guide, for a standard sized shoe box you need about 1m (1⅛yd) of fabric.

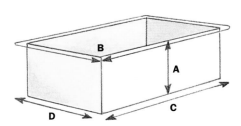

1 Cutting fabric for box *For sides of the box,* measure the depth (**A**) and around outside of box (**B**) and add 2.5cm (1in) to both amounts for turnings. Cut a rectangle of fabric to these measurements. *For base of the box,* measure the box base (**C**) and (**D**), and cut a rectangle of fabric 6mm (¼in) smaller than this all round.

2 Covering sides Spray adhesive on one long side of the box. Smooth the long fabric rectangle along this side of the box with one short edge extending beyond one short side of the box by 1cm (⅜in) and the long edges extending beyond the long sides by 1cm (⅜in). Work round the box, gluing one side at a time.

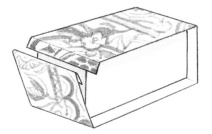

3 Neatening the end When you get to the last side, press under and glue the raw edge so it finishes flush with the box edge, and then stick this side down with spray adhesive.

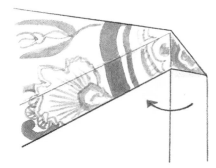

4 Neatening the edges and base Using fabric glue, stick the overlapping fabric to the inside of the box on the top edge. Glue the overlapping fabric on both long edges to the base of the box. Fold the corners of the overlaps on both short edges into neat mitres and glue these down. Spray adhesive over the base of the box and stick the base piece of fabric centrally in place.

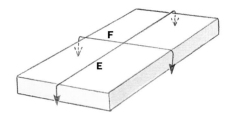

5 Cutting fabric for lid Measure the length (**E**) and width (**F**) of the lid, including the sides, and add 2.5cm (1in) to both measurements. Cut a rectangle of fabric to these dimensions, remembering to centre any prominent motifs in the fabric on the top of the lid.

6 Covering the lid Spray adhesive over the lid and position the fabric centrally on top. Glue down the long sides, then the short sides, tucking in the extra fabric at the corners. Glue the overlapping fabric to the inside.

7 Lining the box (optional) For a neat finish, line the box with pieces of fabric-covered card made to fit the inside walls and base.

Covering a round box

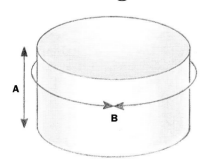

1 Cutting the fabric *For the sides,* measure depth of the box (**A**) and around the outside of the box (**B**), and add 2.5cm (1in) to these dimensions. Cut a rectangle of fabric to this size. *For the base,* place the box on the fabric, draw around it, then cut it out.

2 Covering the sides On one short end of the fabric rectangle, fold 1cm (³⁄₈in) to wrong side and glue in place. Spray the sides of the box with adhesive and smooth the fabric on top, leaving an equal amount of overlap on both top and base edges. Lap the folded edge over raw edge.

3 Neatening the top and base edges On the base edge of the fabric overlap, snip into the fabric all round and glue the flaps of fabric to the base of the box. On the top edge, glue the overlapping fabric to the inside of the box, snipping into the fabric if necessary.

4 Covering the base Trim 6mm (¼in) off the base circle all round, then glue it on to the base of the box.

5 Preparing the lid fabric Cut a strip of fabric to fit around the side of the lid, adding 2cm (¾in) all round for turnings. Place the lid on the paper backing of the Bondaweb; draw around it and roughly cut it out. Sticky side down, fuse the Bondaweb to wrong side of the fabric. Cut out the circle, then peel away the backing paper.

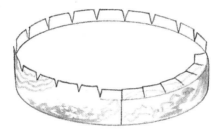

6 Covering the lid side Glue under 1cm (³⁄₈in) on one short side of the fabric. Glue the fabric around the side of the lid, lapping the neatened short end over the raw one. Turn overlapping fabric to the inside of lid and top of the lid. At the top, snip out triangles to reduce bulk, so the turnings lie flat.

7 Covering the lid top Position the fused fabric circle on the lid to check the fit. If necessary, trim a small amount from the edge of the circle, so that it does not extend beyond the edges of the lid. Stick the circle centrally on top of the box.

▼ *If the fabric has a prominent motif, you can make a feature of it by centring it on the top of the lid. The technique for covering a round box can be easily adapted to cover a heart-shaped one — so put the box from those Valentines chocolates to good use!*

Trimming covered boxes

Once you've covered your boxes, why not trim them so they are really special? Here are two different ideas for hand-crafted trims – making small tassels or your own pleated ribbon. For each of these trimmings you can probably raid your sewing kit for the embroidery cotton, ribbon and card required to make them. Alternatively, use purchased trims: pearly beads, glass gemstones, braid or even silk flowers can all be be glued in place to add a decorative flourish.

▲ *The tassel can be attached with a loop of twisted cord, threaded through a hole punched in the box with a bodkin.*

Making a tassel

1 Winding Cut card as wide as desired length of tassel. Wrap embroidery cotton around the card about 20 times. Cut the cotton. Thread a needle with a length of embroidery cotton and pass it under the loops. Remove needle and secure thread ends with a knot.

2 Finishing off Pull the loops off the card. Cut another length of embroidery cotton and wrap it around the loops, about a third of the way down, to form the tassel waist. Tie the ends and use a needle to tuck them inside the tassel. Cut through loops.

Making pleated ribbon

1 Making a template Cut a rectangular card template twice the ribbon width, by the desired finished width of each pleat. Draw a line down the centre of the template.

2 Pinning the pleats Lay the card template, marked side up, over the ribbon at one end, and fold in the ribbon on each side to meet the marked line. Finger press, then slip the template out and pin the pleat in place. Repeat all along the ribbon, leaving no spacing between pleats.

3 Stitching the pleats Tack along centre of ribbon, removing the pins one at a time as you go. Machine stitch along the centre. Unpick the tacking, then glue in place on box lid.

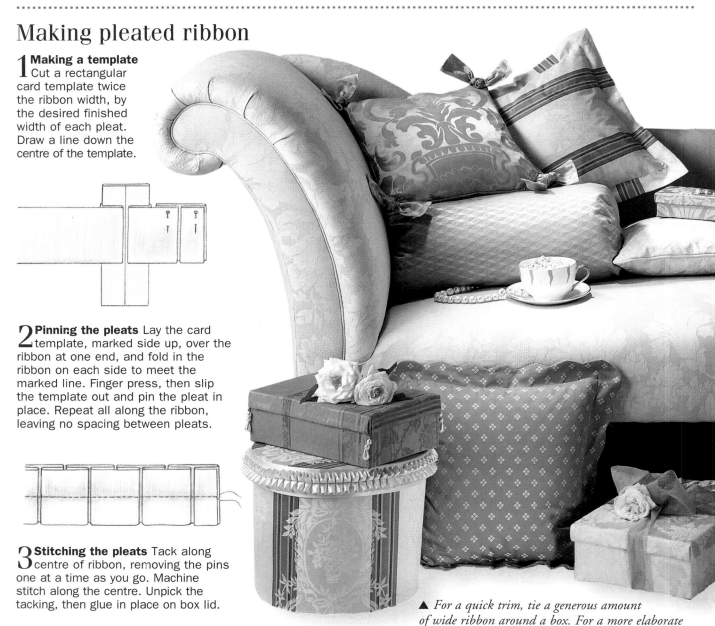

▲ *For a quick trim, tie a generous amount of wide ribbon around a box. For a more elaborate finish, make a pleated ribbon trim (see steps left).*

Covering blanket boxes

*Give a soft, comfortable finish to an old, yet useful, blanket box
with a padded fabric covering. The extra storage space is invaluable
and you gain an attractive piece of furniture too.*

A softly padded, fabric-covered blanket box is an elegant and useful addition to any room. Traditionally placed at the foot of a bed, a blanket box is equally at home in a living room, where it can double as an ottoman – being just the right height for a tray of drinks, or for tired feet! Soft foam padding makes it a comfy place to sit too.

You can revamp an old junkshop find, like the ones on these pages (you'll need to remove any original padding and the staples securing it), or customize a new chest or blanket box. Another cost-saving idea is to make use of coordinating remnants by using different fabrics for the lid, covering and lining. A vibrant braid

▲ *It's amazing just how good an old blanket box can look when it has a bright new cover. If you don't have an old box to re-cover, look out for one at a garage sale or junk shop.*

▶ *You can use the instructions given over the page to cover a box of just about any size and shape – even a small laundry basket like this one.*

adds the finishing touch to the lid.

Make quick work of fixing the fabric by investing in a staple gun – available from do-it-yourself stores. Spray-on adhesive is ideal for fixing the foam and wadding to wood; always work in a well-ventilated area.

Covering a box with fabric

The top of the box is padded with a piece of medium-density, flame-retardant foam – 2.5-5cm (1-2in) deep is suitable. Have your local foam supplier cut the the foam to shape for you. Lightweight wadding is wrapped over the foam and round the sides to soften all the edges before the final fabric layer is added. To comply with safety regulations, make sure you buy a flame-retardant fabric.

You will also need enough braid to go twice round the box. The braid serves a dual purpose – hiding the raw fabric edges as well as being decorative.

You will need

- ◆ **Blanket box**
- ◆ **Fabric for lid**
- ◆ **Fabric for sides**
- ◆ **Braid**
- ◆ **Matching thread, needle and pins**
- ◆ **2.5-5cm (1-2in) thick medium-density foam**
- ◆ **Lightweight wadding**
- ◆ **PVA adhesive**
- ◆ **Hammer, chisel, pincers and sandpaper for removing any original upholstery (for old boxes)**
- ◆ **Staple gun and 10mm (³⁄₈in) staples**
- ◆ **Darning needle or bradawl**
- ◆ **Screwdriver**
- ◆ **Pencil**

1 Preparing an old box Loosen any old staples or tacks by jamming a chisel or screwdriver underneath and hitting the hilt with a hammer; then remove them with pincers. Smooth the surface where they have been removed with sandpaper, if necessary.

2 Sticking the foam in place Draw round the hinges with a pencil and unscrew them. Remove any handle and/or holding chain, marking their positions in the same way. Spray the top of the lid with adhesive and press the foam in place.

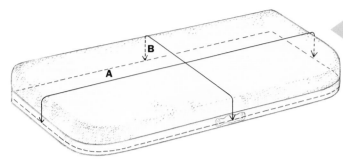

3 Cutting the wadding Measure the length (**A**) and width (**B**) of the padded lid, finishing 1cm (³⁄₈in) from the bottom edge of the lid for each. Cut a piece of wadding **A** by **B**.

4 Stapling the wadding Centre lid, foam side down, on the wadding. At 10cm (4in), then 5cm (2in) intervals, staple wadding to side edges of lid , leaving corners and handle fixings free and pleating round any curves.

5 Finishing the wadding At corners, tuck one edge under to make a vertical pleat; staple in place. Cut away wadding round any fixings and staple the edges. Trim away excess wadding beyond staples all round.

6 Preparing the fabric Measure up for fabric as for wadding (over both foam and wadding), but finishing 6mm (¼in) from the lower edge of the lid. Add 2.5cm (1in) all round and cut out.

7 Fixing the fabric Centre the lid on the wrong side of the fabric, padded side down. Along the back edge, staple the fabric in place just beyond the wadding edge. Pull the front edge tightly over the wadding and put in one centre staple. Repeat on each side, then work outwards along each edge, leaving the corners and curves free.

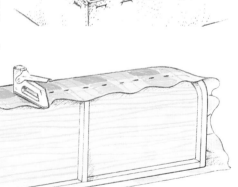

◀ *This is what the blanket box looked like before it was covered.*

8 Neatening the lid Form vertical pleats at corners by tucking one side under the other. Trim excess fabric underneath. Trim fabric close to staples. Starting at centre back, turn under one end of braid, and glue it over fabric edge and staples. At join, turn under end and butt to first.

Covering the sides

1 Positioning the wadding Measure all round the sides of the box and cut a piece of wadding this length by the box height plus 7.5cm (3in). Starting at the centre back, wrap the wadding round the box, with the edges extending equally over the top and base edges of the box, and butting the ends of the wadding together.

2 Stapling the wadding Fold and staple top wadding edge to the inside of the box. Cut away the wadding round the hinge marks, and staple round the edges. Fold and staple the lower edge to the base, neatening the corners and trimming round the feet if necessary.

3 Preparing the fabric Measure round the box sides over the wadding. Cut a piece of fabric this length plus 5cm (2in), by the box height plus 12cm (4¾in). Press under 1.5cm (⅝in) on the long lower edge.

4 Covering the sides Lay the box on its side. Centre wrong side of fabric on the box, with edges extending equally over the top and base edges and with one short edge overlapping a back corner by 2.5cm (1in). Staple along short edge, then wrap the fabric tightly round sides. Turn under remaining short edge in line with corner; pin.

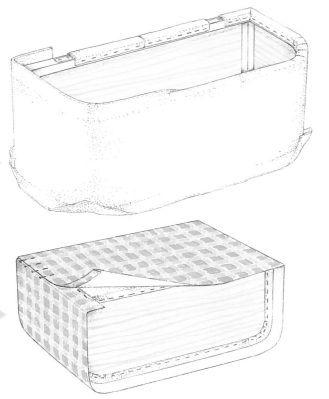

5 Neatening the base edge Staple the folded edge of the fabric to the box base over the wadding, pleating the fabric neatly at the corners and curves.

6 Adding braid At top, transfer hinge marks to fabric. Pull fabric tightly over box edge and staple edge over wadding, pleating at corners and curves. Trim close to staples, and stick braid in place, as in step **8** of the lid.

7 Finishing off Slipstitch pinned corner with matching thread. Replace hinges in marked positions, using a bradawl or darning needle to work holes in fabric for screws.

If you have used coordinating fabrics elsewhere in the room, you can continue the theme in the fabric covering. There is no reason why you must use the same fabric on the lid as the sides of the box – it can be more effective if you don't.

Making a lining

A fabric lining means that precious things are stored free from dust. The lining is tied in place with ribbons, so you can remove it easily for washing. Allow 50cm (20in) of ribbon per bow – on a square box you would need four bows. On a wooden framed box, staples or upholstery nails are used as fixing points for the ties, but cane or bamboo framed boxes usually have gaps in the wickerwork for tying ribbons.

As an alternative way of finishing your box lid, take the fabric over to the inside, cutting away the wadding under the hinges as in *Covering the sides*, step **2**. Pleat the fabric neatly at the corners, and finish with a narrow braid or ribbon.

You will need

- ◆ Lining fabric
- ◆ Backing fabric
- ◆ Matching thread
- ◆ Narrow ribbon
- ◆ Upholstery nails, hammer
- ◆ Paper for template, pencil

▼ *Old wicker and wooden boxes can be quite rough, even grubby, inside. Adding a lining is a good option in this case.*

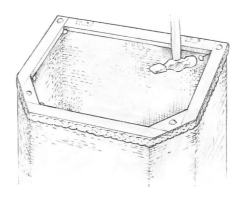

1 Fixing upholstery nails Using the hammer, fix one nail to each inner corner of the box, near to the top. (This step will not be necessary for cane or bamboo boxes.)

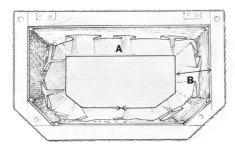

2 Making a template Push a piece of paper down into the box and draw the outline of the base with a pencil. Remove the paper and cut round the outline. Measure round the edge of the template and add 3cm (1¼in) (**A**). Measure the inside height of the box and add 3cm (1¼in) (**B**).

3 Cutting out *For the base:* cut one piece from the template from both the lining and backing, adding 1.5cm (⅝in) all round for seams. *For the sides:* cut one piece from both the lining and backing measuring **A** times **B**.

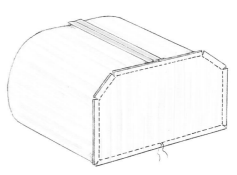

4 Stitching the lining Pin the two short edges of side lining piece right sides together; stitch, then press the seam open. Right sides and raw edges together, pin one edge of side lining to edges of lining base, centring the seam on the back edge of the base, and clipping at corners. Stitch.

5 Adding the ties Cut the ribbon into 50cm (20in) lengths and fold in half. Place the lining in the box and mark each nail position on the right side of the fabric. Pin the folded ribbons in place at each mark, with the fold of each ribbon level with the raw edge of the lining. Tack in place.

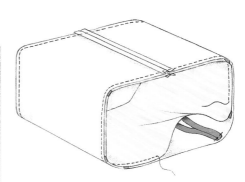

6 Adding the backing Make up the backing in the same way as the lining. Right sides and raw edges together, pin the top edges of the lining and backing together, matching the side seam and sandwiching the ribbons between. Stitch, leaving a 15cm (6in) gap for turning through.

7 Finishing off Turn to right side, press, and topstitch all round the top edge close to the fold, catching in the edges of the opening. Loop the ties round the nails and tie in bows.

Slip-on headboard cover

*A simple slip-on cover is a great way to smarten
up an old upholstered headboard. You can make it in a fabric to
coordinate with the room, and remove it easily for washing.*

Re-upholstering a headboard may seem a somewhat daunting task, but it's a shame to throw away an old headboard just because it's a bit tatty or clashes with a new colour scheme. A neatly piped, slip-on cover can be the answer – it's simple to make and easy to remove for cleaning. The cover is lightly padded with wadding and lined, and is shaped to fit the headboard. Even if your headboard is already padded, the wadding gives a smoother finish, but you can omit it if your fabric is quite substantial in weight.

Contrast piping around the edges of the cover gives a crisp finish. If you have a thick headboard, you can add a gusset between the front and back panels of

▲ *The dramatic, Gothic shape of this headboard is accentuated by the strong check of the fabric cover. The depth of the headboard means that it is best made with a separate gusset.*

the basic pattern. The back of the cover is split down the centre and fastened with ties, making it quick to fit.

Making a slip-on headboard cover

Most furnishing fabrics are not wide enough for queen and king size headboards. In these cases, use a full width for the cover and join a strip on to each selvedge edge to make up the width; this avoids an unsightly seam down the centre. You can use sheeting fabric for the lining, which comes in wider widths.

▶ *This method works for covering a headboard of any shape, even an ogee-shaped one like this. Here, a bold fabric print is shown off to full advantage.*

You will need

- ◆ **Headboard**
- ◆ **Furnishing fabric**
- ◆ **Fabric for piping**
- ◆ **Lining fabric**
- ◆ **Mediumweight wadding**
- ◆ **Matching thread**
- ◆ **Piping cord**
- ◆ **Large sheet of paper, pen**
- ◆ **Pins**

Fabric quantities

Check the chart below to work out the materials you'll need. Amounts are based on furnishing fabric 140cm (54in) wide, lining fabric (sheeting) 229cm (90in) wide and wadding 90cm (35in) wide.

Bed size	Main fabric	Lining	Wadding
Single 91cm (3ft)	2 widths x **A**	2 widths x **A**	3 widths x **A**
Double 136cm (4ft 6in)	3 widths x **A**	2 widths x **A**	4 widths x **A**
Queen 151cm (5ft)	3 widths x **A**	2 widths x **A**	4 widths x **A**
King 195cm (6ft 6in)	3 widths x **A**	2 widths x **A**	4 widths x **A**

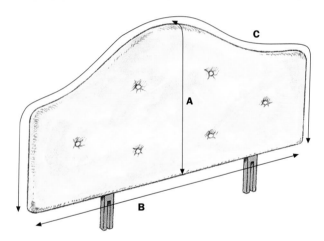

1 Measuring up *For the length* (**A**), measure from the top of the headboard to the bottom edge and add 10cm (4in). *For the width* (**B**), measure the width of your headboard and choose the corresponding size on the *Fabric quantities* chart. *For piping cord* (**C**), measure along the sides and top and add 10cm (4in).

2 Making a pattern Remove the headboard from the bed base and place it, face down, on top of the paper. Use the pen to draw around the headboard; add 2.5cm (1in) all round to allow for the thickness of the wadding and the seam allowances, graduating to 3.5cm (1³⁄₈in) at the sides to allow for the struts at the back of the headboard. Cut out the pattern.

3 Cutting out the cover front Join strips to each side of a full width of the main fabric, as necessary, to make up the required width for the cover front; press seams open. To join the wadding, butt the edges together and make diagonal tacking stitches across the join. Use the pattern to cut out one front piece from each of the main fabric, wadding and lining.

4 Cutting out back Fold pattern in half and place centre fold 1.5cm (⁵⁄₈in) away from a straight edge of wadding. Cut two pieces of wadding to this shape. With the fabric folded double, repeat to cut back pieces from lining and main fabric. Cut along fold to make two back pieces of each.

5 Applying piping Cut out and make up piping. Pin front fabric piece right side up to front wadding piece and apply piping along the sides and top edge.

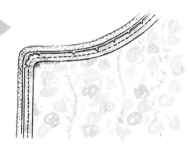

6 Preparing back For the back of the cover, pin each back main fabric piece, right side up to a back wadding piece. Then, with right sides together, pin the two halves of the back along the centre edge. Machine stitch 5cm (2in) down from the top edge and press the seam open.

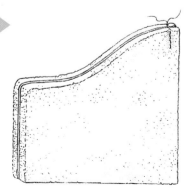

7 Joining the front and back Right sides together, pin the back to the front piece, matching the raw edges on the sides and top. Stitch along sides and top.

8 Making up the lining Pin the two halves of the back, right sides together, and stitch 5cm (2in) down from the top edge. Press the seam open. Right sides together, pin the back and front pieces of the lining together and stitch along the sides and top.

9 Making the ties Cut eight 7 x 40cm (2¾ x 15¾in) strips of fabric. Press under 1cm (⅜in) along each long and one short edge. Fold each strip in half lengthways, wrong sides together and matching folded edges. Stitch close to the edge along the folded sides.

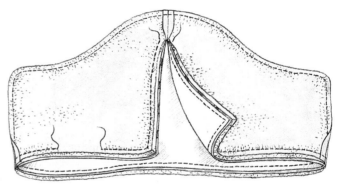

11 Stitching in the lining With right sides together and matching side seams, pin the lining and wadded fabric together at back opening and along the bottom edge, leaving a 20cm (8in) gap along bottom edge at back. Machine stitch round all edges.

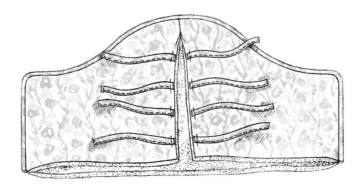

10 Inserting the ties at centre back opening With the back piece right side up and raw edges matching, pin the ties to the main fabric at the centre back opening, as follows: on each side, position the first tie 5cm (2in) up from the bottom edge and place the other three ties equal distances apart. Tack across the ends of the ties to secure in place and remove the pins.

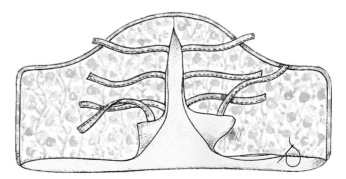

12 Finishing off Turn the cover to right side through the opening and push the lining up inside the cover. Turn in the raw edges and slipstitch opening closed. Press. Slip the cover over the headboard, securing it neatly in place with the ties.

A gusseted headboard cover

If your headboard is deeply upholstered, a headboard cover with a gusset is the best choice for a good fit. It is made in a similar way to the one on the previous page, but has a narrow strip of fabric inserted between the front and back, neatly edged with piping on both sides.

If your fabric has an obvious pattern, you should cut the gusset across the width of the fabric rather than down the length. Multiply **C** twice to work out how much piping cord you need.

1 Measuring up and cutting out Cut out front and back pieces in fabric, wadding and lining, and cut out and make up the ties, as in steps **1-4** and **9** on pages 58 and 59.

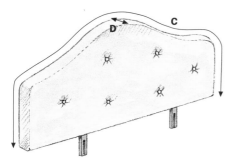

2 Cutting out the gusset Measure the thickness of your headboard (**D**) – 5cm (2in) is usually enough – and add 3cm (1¼in) for seam allowances. Cut a piece of fabric **D** wide, by **C** long, joining strips if necessary to make the required length. Cut a piece of wadding and lining the same size.

3 Making the piping Cut out and make up enough piping to go twice round the sides and the top of the headboard.

4 Preparing the front and back Make up the front and back pieces of the cover, as in steps **5-6**, on page 58. Apply the piping to the sides and top edge of the front and the back pieces.

5 Adding the gusset Right side up, pin the gusset main fabric piece to the gusset wadding piece and mark the centre point along both edges. Then mark the centre of the front and back pieces at the top edge. Right sides together and matching the centre marks and raw edges, pin the gusset along the top and sides of the front piece. Stitch together, taking a 1.5cm (⅝in) seam allowance. Repeat to join the other side of the gusset to the back piece.

6 Completing the cover Make up the lining back pieces, as in step **8** on the previous page. Join front and back lining pieces together, inserting the lining gusset as for the main cover in step **5**, below left. Stitch in the lining, adding the ties, and finish off, as in steps **10-12** on the previous page.

▲ *Even when covered in self-fabric, piping adds shape and definition to a headboard cover. If the fabric has a large motif, try to position it centrally on the cover, as here.*

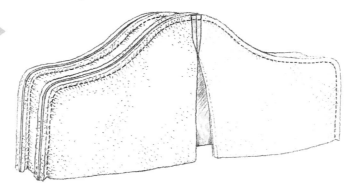

Upholstered headboards

*A thickly padded and upholstered headboard makes a luxurious
addition to any bedroom. It has an inviting softness, ideal for sitting
up in bed, and gives a carefully finished, tailored look.*

Making your own traditional-style, upholstered headboard is a very economical way of achieving a glamorous, elegant finish for your bedroom. Interesting details, such as contrast piping and a ruched border, offer the opportunity to emphasize the colour scheme of the room.

The headboard base should be cut from medium density fibreboard, plywood or good quality chipboard. Designing your own shape is fun, but even a plain rectangle looks good. Alternatively, you could strip down an old headboard and make a new cover for it. Use the old fabric pieces as a pattern.

The board itself is covered with a layer of thick foam, and the central fabric panel is stapled on to the foam. A row of piping and a ruched border are added, and then the back is finished with lining fabric. Very little sewing is involved – simply for making up the piping and the gathered border strip.

Choose mediumweight, closely woven furnishing fabrics to coordinate with your bedroom – patterned fabrics are best as they show marks less than plain ones. Since the fabrics are permanently stapled on to the board, it's a good idea to finish your headboard with a spray-on fabric protector to prevent staining.

▼ *Here, a swirly, floral print is prettily complemented by the curvy shape of the headboard and the ruched border.*

Making the headboard

A headboard is usually about 50-69cm (20-27in) high, measured from the top of the mattress. For the width, measure across the bed and add 10-15cm (4-6in) to each side to allow for bedding.

When buying foam, ensure that it is flame retardant; allow the size of the headboard plus 5cm (2in) all round.

You need one specialist material, called backtacking strip. This narrow cardboard strip gives a smooth, firm base to staple the fabrics on to. Allow the width plus twice the height of the board. It is available from upholstery suppliers, or you could ask your local upholsterer to sell you some.

When stapling along a line, space the staples at regular intervals, so you can stagger them for each layer.

For details on fixing your headboard to the bed, see overleaf.

You will need

- ◆ **Fabrics for centre panel, piping and border**
- ◆ **Mediumweight wadding**
- ◆ **Lining fabric for back**
- ◆ **Matching thread**
- ◆ **Piping cord**
- ◆ **Thin cord for gathering border**
- ◆ **13mm (½in) thick MDF plywood or chipboard**
- ◆ **Panel saw and coping saw**
- ◆ **4cm (1½in) thick foam**
- ◆ **All purpose adhesive**
- ◆ **Staple gun and 13mm (½in) staples**
- ◆ **Backtacking strip**
- ◆ **Paper for pattern**
- ◆ **Pencil**
- ◆ **Scissors**
- ◆ **Felt tip pen**
- ◆ **Cording foot (optional)**

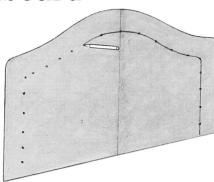

1 Designing the shape Cut a piece of paper to the finished width and height of your headboard. Fold the paper in half widthways and draw your chosen shape on to it. Unfold the pattern to check the shape, then cut it out. *For the border:* measure in and mark 10cm (4in) round the sides and top, and join in a smooth line.

2 Cutting the board and foam Lay the pattern on the board and draw round it. Use the panel saw to cut the straight lines and the coping saw to cut the curves. Lay the board on the foam, with the lower edges level; cut the foam 5cm (2in) larger all round the sides and top.

3 Securing the foam Spread adhesive on the face of the board. With the lower edges level, press the foam on top of the board. Pull the excess foam around the sides and base of the board and staple it to the back of the board with the staple gun.

4 Marking the border Trim away the border from the paper pattern. Centre the paper pattern on the board, matching the lower edges; then use the felt tip pen to draw round it on to the foam.

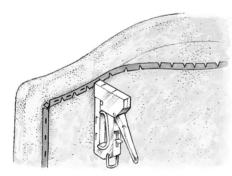

5 Stapling the backtacking Starting at the bottom edge, lay one edge of the strip along marked line; staple in centre of strip, through the foam to the board. Work along strip, stapling at 5cm (2in) intervals and clipping the edge to ease it around any curves.

6 Cutting out the main fabric Cut a rectangle of fabric 4cm (1½in) bigger all round than the inner panel. If the fabric is not wide enough, join strips on either side of a width and press the seams open.

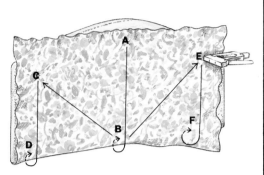

7 Positioning the inner panel Centre the fabric right side up over the inner panel. Staple the fabric to the backtacking strip, first at the top centre (**A**), then on the back at the bottom (**B**). Then staple one corner of the fabric (**C**), and then the lower edge below it (**D**). Repeat for the other side (**E** and **F**).

8 Securing the inner panel Fill in with staples at 5cm (2in) intervals along the backtacking strip, and on the back along the lower edge. Then trim the excess fabric to 1.5cm (⅝in).

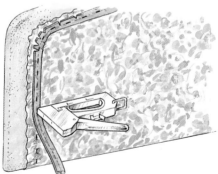

9 Adding the piping Cut and make up piping to the length of backtacking strip plus 10cm (4in). Leaving a 5cm (2in) loose end and with the raw edges facing out, centre the seamline of the piping along the line of staples. Staple at 5cm (2in) intervals, clipping around curves. Staple ends at back.

10 Cutting the border Measure around the side and top edges of the board. In the border fabric, cut strips across the fabric 15cm (6in) wider than the finished border width. Join them to make a strip 2½-3 times longer than outer edge of headboard.

Using a different print for the border makes an interesting contrast to accentuate a colour scheme. Piping adds a finishing touch.

11 Gathering the border Leaving 5cm (2in) ungathered at each end, lay the thin cord 1cm (⅜in) in from one long edge of the border strip. Using a cording foot on your sewing machine if you have one, work a long zigzag stitch over the cord. Divide and mark the fabric strip into quarters; then carefully pull the cord through the zigzagging to gather it up to fit the line of piping on the board.

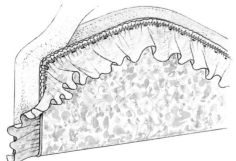

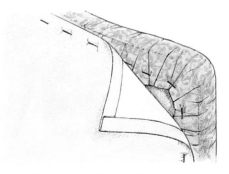

12 Attaching border Divide piping on board into quarters and mark. Right sides and raw edges together and matching marks, lay gathered edge of strip over piping. Staple at the marks; adjust gathers, giving extra fullness at corners. Complete stapling.

13 Finishing the border Cut a strip of wadding the width of the border plus 4cm (1½in). Wrap over the front and edge of the border under the ruched fabric, as shown. Pull border fabric over wadding to back of board; adjust the gathers and staple in place.

14 Neatening the back Use the headboard as a template to cut a piece of lining. Press under 12mm (½in) all round the outside edges. Position the lining right side out on the back of the headboard, to cover all the raw edges; staple in place.

Fixing a headboard

On most beds the headboard is screwed to two strong wooden battens, which are then fixed to the base of the bed with large bolts. The bolts are positioned about 15cm (6in) in from the sides and about halfway down the base.

If the base does not have bolts for fixing the headboard, you can use metal plates to fix it directly to the wall. The plates slot together, holding the headboard flush against the wall. This method is also a useful solution for tall or heavy headboards, which tend to rattle about.

Fixing to the bed

You will need two pieces of 45 x 20mm (1¾ x ¾in) wooden batten, 800mm (31½in) long, a pencil, drill, wood twist bit and four woodscrews.

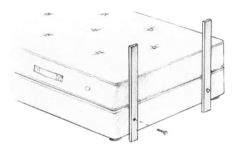

1 Drilling bolt holes Remove the bolts from the bed base. Stand the battens on the floor against the bed base; mark height of bolt holes on back of each. Drill a hole at each marked point large enough to take the bolt. Bolt the battens temporarily on to the bed.

2 Positioning headboard Centre the headboard on the bed against the battens; draw around the battens on back of headboard. On the battens, mark the position of the bottom edge of the headboard, then unbolt them.

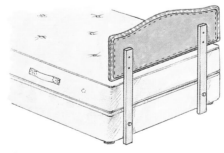

3 Fixing the battens On each batten, drill two holes for the woodscrews, positioning them above the mark that indicates the base of the headboard. Then, with the headboard face down and matching the marks, screw the battens to the back of it. Finally, bolt the headboard on to the bed.

Making a double piped headboard

For a neat finish, add a second row of piping around the top of the headboard. You will need enough extra piping to go round the sides and top edge, plus 5cm (2in).

Follow steps **1-13** on the previous pages. Then neaten the ends of the piping and position it on the edge of the board, with the raw edges lying flat on the back. Staple the piping in place all round, just below the stitching line. Then use the headboard as a template to cut out the lining, adding on 12mm (½in) all round. Press in the allowance, then staple it on to the back, covering the raw edges.

Fixing to the wall

You will need two sets of slot plates, a drill and drill bit, wall plugs, screws and screwdriver. You will also need ink or chalk to mark the position of the screws on the headboard.

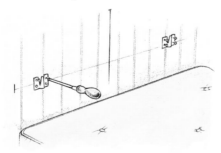

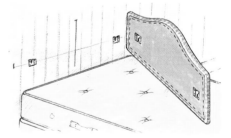

1 Positioning the slot plates Prop the headboard in position on the mattress. On the wall, mark the centre top of the headboard and the centre of one side edge; remove the headboard and draw a vertical line down the wall from the centre mark. On either side of the line, and level with the side edge mark, fix one half of each pair of slot plates, tongues pointing up; leave the screws 6mm (¼in) proud of the wall.

2 Fixing the headboard Rub chalk or ink on to the screw heads. Then, with the headboard in the correct position, press it against the screws so that the ink or chalk marks the back. Fix the other half of the plates at the marks, with the tongues pointing down, then drop the headboard on to the fixings.

Duvet cover and pillowcases

*Making your own matching duvet (comforter) cover and
pillowcases to complement your bedroom scheme is a real
boon, both in design terms and as a financial saving.*

Because of its size and position on
the bed, a duvet cover makes a
powerful design contribution in
a bedroom. But sometimes it can be
surprisingly tricky and costly to find
precisely the correct pattern in the right
colourway to go with your current
room scheme.

Making up a duvet cover yourself is
an excellent way round such a problem.
Although you are working with large
amounts of fabric, the actual sewing is
quite straightforward – it only involves
stitching long, straight seams. You can
also pick an inexpensive cotton or polyester-cotton in a colour and pattern to
suit your bedroom decorations exactly.

To double the decorative value of a
duvet cover, you can make it reversible
by using a different fabric for each side.
For the best effect, choose two coordinating fabrics that are linked by colour
or pattern, or both.

Once you have made your duvet
cover, you can sew matching or toning
pillowcases to complete the picture.

▲ *Making the opposite sides of a duvet
cover in lively, coordinating patterns,
with pillowcases to match, focuses
maximum attention on the bed. For
extra impact, you can insert a deep frill
into each pillowcase as you sew it.*

Making a duvet cover

A duvet cover is basically a very simple rectangular bag, fastened along one edge. There are many ingenious ways of holding the opening closed – you can sew on a series of ties, for example, or a row of buttons – but the easiest and neatest is with press-fastener tape, which you can buy by the metre from sewing stores.

To neaten the raw edges of the seams inside and strengthen the cover, you sew the duvet cover together with enclosed, double seams called French seams, that are quick to work.

Choosing fabric

Pure cotton or polyester-cotton mixes are a practical choice as they are machine washable and reasonably priced. You can buy 230cm (90in) wide polycotton sheeting in a wide range of plain colours and coordinating designs. A 280cm (110in) wide cotton is also available if your duvet is extra large. See pages 77–80 for more details.

If you want to use a narrower fabric to match or coordinate with other patterns already in the room, you can join fabric widths to make up the required width. To avoid an unsightly seam down the centre of the cover, add two strips on either side of a full width.

SIZE WISE CHART

Check the size of your duvet carefully before buying your fabric. Standard sizes for duvets are:

Size	Width		Length	
	cm	In	cm	In
Single	135	54	200	78
Double	200	78	200	78
King size	230	90	220	86
Super king	260	102	220	86

You will need

- ◆ **Sheeting fabric – twice the length of your duvet plus 14cm (5¹⁄₂in)**
- ◆ **Press-fastener tape – 100cm (39¹⁄₂in) for single, 150cm (59in) for double, 160cm (63in) for king or super-king size bed**
- ◆ **Matching thread**
- ◆ **Pins and Scissors**
- ◆ **Dressmaker's pencil**

▼ *Using different sized checks on the two sides of a duvet cover offsets a flamboyant floral bed valance perfectly.*

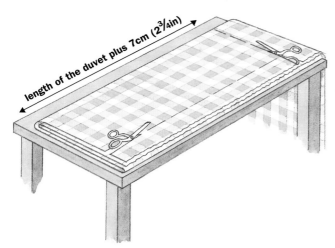

1 Cutting out Square up the raw edges of one piece of fabric against a straight edge. To make it easier to manage such wide fabric, fold the width in half and half again before cutting out. From one raw edge, measure the length of the duvet plus 7cm (2¾in). Mark with a dressmaker's pencil and cut in a straight line through each layer of fabric in turn. Trim the width to the width of the duvet plus 4cm (1½in). Cut the other piece of fabric to the same size.

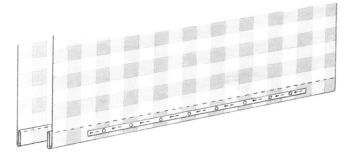

2 Positioning the fastener tape Press under a double 2.5cm (1in) hem along the lower edge of each piece and machine stitch close to the inner fold. Separate the two sides of the press-fastener tape. Centre one side along the hem on the right side of each cover piece and pin in place.

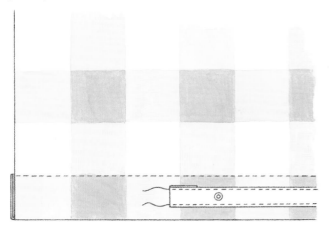

3 Stitching the fastener tape Lay the two cover pieces together, pressing the fasteners closed to check that the two sides correspond exactly, and adjust the position of the tape if necessary. Undo the fasteners carefully. Turn under the raw ends of the tape by 1cm (⅜in) and, using a zipper foot, machine stitch both long edges, close to the edge of the tape.

4 Starting a French seam Position the two cover pieces wrong sides together, aligning the press fasteners without doing them up. Pin then stitch the two sides and base of the duvet cover, taking a 1cm (⅜in) seam. Trim the seam allowance to 6mm (¼in).

5 Finishing the French seam Turn the cover out to the wrong side, press the sides and stitch round the edges again, 1cm (⅜in) in, to enclose the raw edges. Clip the two sides of the press fastener tape together.

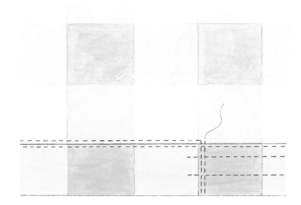

6 Completing the opening At each end of the tape, pin the two cover pieces together just above the hem, from the seams to 1.5cm (⅝in) beyond the ends of the tape. Then pin at right angles across the hem and tape to the edge. Machine stitch the pinned lines, reverse stitching across the width of the hem to strengthen it. Turn the duvet cover right side out.

Making a pillowcase

You can make plain pillowcases to match or coordinate with your duvet cover quite simply. A standard pillow is 46cm (18in) wide by 71cm (28in) long, so 1m (1⅛yd) of sheeting is enough to make a pair of pillowcases. Check your pillows are a standard size first.

Alternatively, use plain cotton fabric. As it is narrower than sheeting, you need 1.7m (2yd) of 112cm (42in) wide cotton, which is enough for two.

▶ *A set of pillowcases to match the duvet cover completes a stylish bed treatment of your own design.*

You will need

For one pillowcase:

◆ **50cm (¾yd) sheeting fabric**

◆ **Matching thread**

◆ **Scissors**

◆ **Pins**

1 Cutting out Cut out a rectangle of fabric twice the length of the pillow plus 24cm (9½in) (**A**) by the width of the pillow plus 4cm (1½in) (**B**). Aim to position a main motif so that it is centred on one side of the pillowcase once it is folded and stitched.

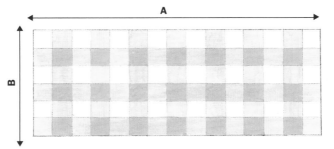

ADD APPLIQUE **Tip**
Instead of making pillowcases from a fabric to match or coordinate with the duvet, you can use a plain fabric and appliqué a motif or motifs cut out from the duvet fabric on to one corner or along an edge.

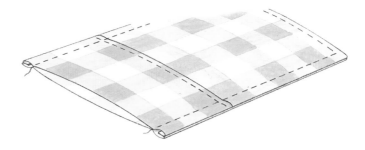

2 Sewing the hems Press under and machine a double 1cm (⅜in) hem on one short end. On the other short end, press under a 6mm (¼in) turning, then 3.5cm (1⅜in) and machine stitch. Bringing wrong sides together, fold and press under the 3.5cm (1⅜in) hem end by 15cm (6in). Fold the 1cm (⅜in) hemmed edge to meet the pressed edge with right sides out.

3 Completing the pillowcase Pin and stitch the raw edges, taking a 1cm (⅜in) seam. Trim seams to 6mm (¼in). Turn the pillowcase to the wrong side, press flat and stitch a 1cm (⅜in) seam to enclose raw edges. Turn the case to the right side and press to finish.

Frilled duvet cover

*Bring a touch of romance into your bedroom by
adding a deep and luxurious frill round the edge of
your duvet (comforter) cover and matching pillowcase.*

Adding a gathered frill to a basic duvet cover is very easy and straightforward, giving it a distinct style all its own. For a really coordinated look, you can make pillowcases to match. Simply hem the edge of the frill or, better still, make a double-sided frill, giving you a duvet that looks equally good from both sides. You can use the same fabric as the cover, or add interest and detail by making the frill in a contrasting fabric. Add a floral frill to a striped duvet, or use a plain, bold colour to set off a jazzy pattern. You can also vary the width of the frill: a narrow frill gives a crisp, neat finish, while a

▲ *Make a dramatic statement by choosing a bold, floral print and adding a deep, flouncy frill to a matching duvet cover and pillowcase.*

deep one looks soft and feminine. Add the frill to the sides and lower edge only, or stitch it all the way round the cover.

Making a cover with a double-sided frill

The instructions given here show how to make a cover to fit a duvet of any size, trimmed with a 10cm (4in) wide double-sided frill.

You will need

- Fabric for the cover
- Fabric for the frill
- Matching thread
- Press-fastener tape
- Pins
- Scissors

1 Cutting out the cover *For the back:* cut one piece the width of the duvet plus 3cm (1¼in) by the length plus 6.5cm (2⅝in). *For the front:* cut one piece 1.5cm (⅝in) bigger all round than the duvet. *For the facing:* cut a strip the width of the front by 5cm (2in).

2 Cutting out the frill *For the frill:* measure around the four sides of the duvet and multiply this measurement by one and a half. Cut enough 23cm (9¼in) wide strips in your chosen frill fabric to make up this length.

3 Making the frill With right sides together, join all frill strips to make a loop. Press seams open, then fold the joined strips in half with wrong sides and raw edges together. Press. Divide loop into four equal sections and mark with pins on the raw edges.

4 Gathering the frill Starting and stopping at the marked pins, stitch two rows of gathering threads along the raw edge, positioning one row 1.2cm (½in) from the raw edge, and then a second row stitched 6mm (¼in) from the edge.

The advantage of making your own duvet cover is that you can make a generous, deep frill for a luxurious effect.

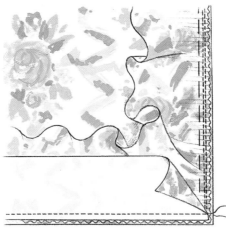

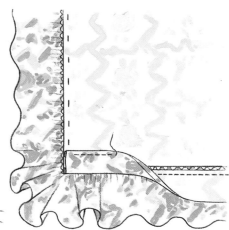

5 Attaching the frill Mark the centre of each side of the front piece with pins. With the pins and raw edges matching, pin frill to right side of front piece. Gather frill to fit, easing extra fullness into the corners. Tack the frill in place, taking 1.5cm (⅝in) seams.

6 Attaching the facing With right sides together, pin the facing to one short end of the front piece, with the frill sandwiched between the two layers. Machine stitch in place, taking a 1.5cm (⅝in) seam allowance.

7 Neatening opening Fold under 1cm (⅜in) of facing. Turn to wrong side. Stitch close to fold, taking care not to catch frill in stitching and stopping 1.5cm (⅝in) from side edges. Turn under and stitch a double 2.5cm (1in) hem on one short side of back piece.

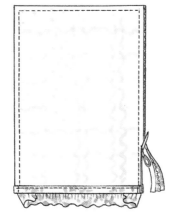

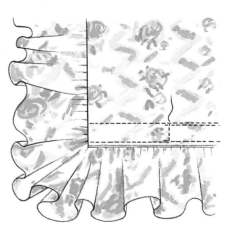

8 Stitching the seams Prepare and attach fastener tape. Pin front and back pieces, right sides together, sandwiching the frill between and matching hemmed short edge to facing. Stitch sides and unhemmed short edge, taking a 1.5cm (⅝in) seam, keeping frill out of way. Trim seams and zigzag to neaten. Turn to right side.

9 Finishing the opening Press the fasteners closed. Pin together the remaining sections of the opening and stitch close to the fold through all the layers, from each side seam to the beginning of the fastener tape. Pivot the needle, as necessary, to stitch across the allowances for the opening, catching in the ends of the tape.

Making a duvet cover with a hemmed frill

If the fabric for your frill is heavier than that of the cover, or you don't have enough for a double-sided frill, simply hem the edges. You'll need the same materials as before, but slightly less fabric to make the frill. Adapt the instructions for making the cover as follows:

1 Cutting out *For cover:* follow step **1** for cutting out back, front and facing pieces. *For frill:* measure around duvet as in step **2**; cut enough 14.5cm (5⅜in) wide strips to make this length.

2 Stitching frill Right sides together, join all strips for frill to make a loop. Neaten seam allowances and press seams open. Turn under a double 1cm (⅜in) hem to wrong side; machine stitch in place close to fold. Divide loop into four equal sections; mark with pins along the raw edge.

3 Completing the cover Continue making up the cover following steps **4-9** of *Making a cover with a double-sided frill,* working the gathering threads along raw edge of frill only.

Making a frilled pillowcase

A matching or coordinating pillowcase completes the bedding ensemble. Plain pillowcases are simple to sew and a frill is an easy and attractive addition. These instructions are for a 7.5cm (3in) frill.

You will need

- ◆ Fabric for pillowcase
- ◆ Fabric for frill or use a ready-made lace frill
- ◆ Matching thread
- ◆ Scissors, pins

1 Cutting out *For the front and back pieces:* cut two rectangles of fabric the width of the pillow plus 3cm (1¼in) by the length plus 3cm (1¼in). Cut a separate flap, 20cm (8in) deep by the width of the pillow plus 3cm (1¼in).

2 Making the frill Measure the four sides of the pillow and multiply this measurement by one and a half. Cut enough 18cm (7¼in) wide strips and join with right sides together to make up this length. Press seams open, then fold the strips in half with wrong sides and raw edges together. Divide the loop into four equal sections and mark with pins along the raw edges.

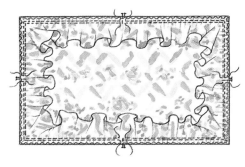

3 Attaching the frill Follow steps **4** and **5** on pages 70–71 for details on gathering the frill and tacking it to the right side of the pillowcase front piece.

4 Stitching the pillowcase Stitch a double 1.5cm (⅝in) hem on one short end of the back piece. Stitch a double 1cm (⅜in) hem on one long edge of the flap. With right sides together and raw edges even, place the back and front together. Position flap, right side down, over the back hemmed edge, matching front and flap raw edges. Stitch outer edges.

5 Completing the pillowcase Remove tacking stitches, then trim the seam allowances and snip across corners to reduce bulk. Zigzag stitch seams to neaten. Turn through to right side and press. Insert pillow.

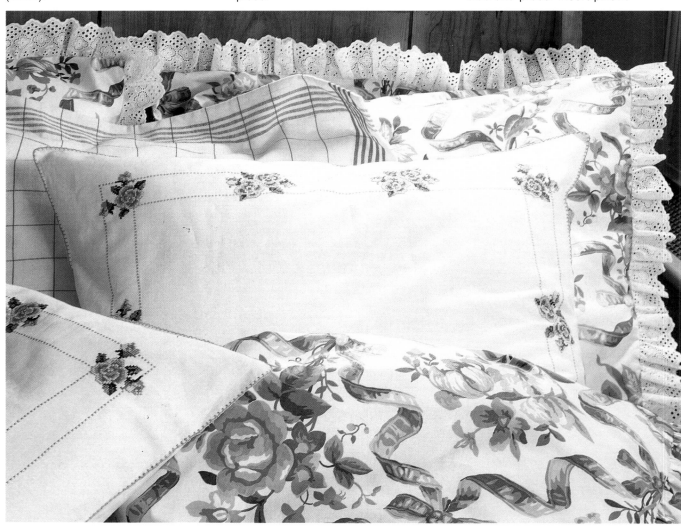

Gathered bed valance

A prettily ruffled valance sets off a beautiful quilt or duvet (comforter) cover perfectly, especially when you choose fabric to complement your existing bedlinen or room setting.

The graceful folds of a gathered valance add the final touch to the best-dressed beds, concealing the bed base, legs, or any storage space beneath the bed. While sheeting valances are readily available in the shops, it's sometimes difficult to find the right shade or pattern to suit your chosen room scheme. The ideal solution is to make your own – you can use the same fabric as the duvet cover or pick a different, complementary pattern that works well with the rest of your bedlinen. You can make one in a tiny floral

cotton to flatter a pretty antique quilt, use a crisp check to enliven a multi-floral room or a striped fabric to make the bed seem higher.

To make the skirt of the valance, you can use a light or mediumweight furnishing fabric that hangs in natural folds. Since only the skirt is visible, you can make the top panel, which goes over the bed base, from very inexpensive sheeting or lining fabric. Where the top panel might be seen over the edge of the bed base, it is bordered with fabric to match the skirt, for a professional finish.

▲ *Ever since duvets became the favoured bedding in most bedrooms, an evenly gathered, coordinated bed valance, like the one above, has come into its own for bridging the gap from mattress to floor.*

Making a gathered bed valance

A bed valance fits neatly over the bed base, with a decorative skirt hanging over the foot of the bed and down on either side. Continuing the skirt a short way round the head end of the bed base ensures that the valance stays firmly in place. When measuring up, remove the mattress and run the tape from side to side and end to end of the bed base itself – the mattress measurements may differ from the bed base slightly. For the drop, make sure the gathered skirt just clears, rather than touches, the floor, so that the folds hang freely.

The skirt is made up from strips cut across the width of the fabric so that any pattern shows clearly. When buying fabric, remember to allow for pattern repeat. You'll need less fabric if you use sheeting, as it comes in wider widths. (See pages 77–80 for more details.)

You will need

- ◆ Furnishing fabric – approximately 4.5m (5yd) for a single bed, 5m (5½yd) for a double bed
- ◆ Sheeting fabric – approximately 1m (1⅛yd) for a single bed, 2m (2¼yd) for a double bed
- ◆ Matching thread
- ◆ Tape measure
- ◆ Scissors
- ◆ Pins
- ◆ Saucer or small plate
- ◆ Dressmaker's pencil

1 Measuring up *For the top panel:* measure the width of the bed base (**A**) and the length (**B**). *For the depth of the frill:* measure the drop from the top of the bed base to just above the floor (**C**).

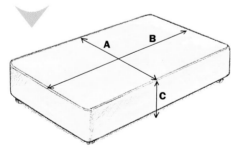

2 Cutting the top panel *For the top:* add 3cm (1¼in) to both **A** and **B** and cut one piece from sheeting.

3 Cutting out the border *For side borders:* cut two 12.5cm (5¼in) wide strips of furnishing fabric the length of the sheeting for the top panel. Join the strips together if necessary, taking a 1.5cm (⅝in) seam allowance, and press seams open. *For end borders:* cut two strips to fit between the side strips at each end, plus 3cm (1¼in).

4 Cutting out the skirt For the total width of the skirt, add **A** to twice **B** and double it, to allow for the gathering. Divide this amount by the width of your furnishing fabric to find out how many widths you need. Cut out the required number of widths, by **C** plus 8cm (3¼in) for seams and hem allowance.

5 Adding borders Press under 1.5cm (⅝in) along one long edge of all border strips. Then, right sides up and matching raw edges, pin and tack one side border to each long edge of the top panel. Pin and tack end borders in place, slipping the raw edge at each end under the side borders.

6 Stitching borders Trim off any excess fabric, then machine stitch close to folded edge along all pressed edges. Tack raw edges of border and top panel together and treat the two layers as one in the following steps.

7 Rounding the corners Place the saucer upside down on one corner of the top panel, aligning the rim of the saucer with the raw edges of the border and top panel. Draw around the saucer to curve the corner, then cut along the line. Repeat for the other three corners.

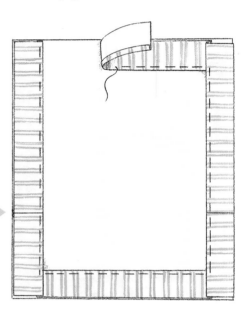

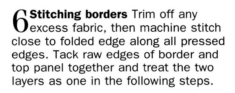

6.5cm (2⅝in)

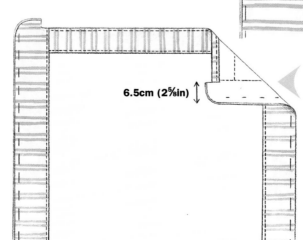

8 Hemming top end On one short side of the top panel, mark and snip the fabric 6.5cm (2⅝in) from each side. Between these two points, press the 1.5cm (⅝in) seam allowance to the wrong side, then tuck the raw edge in to make a narrow hem. Machine stitch close to the folded edge.

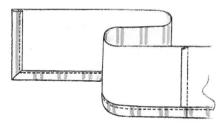

9 Joining the skirt widths Join all the widths using French seams to make one long strip. Take care to match the pattern direction on all pieces. On the bottom and side edges, press under a 1.5cm (⅝in), then 5cm (2in), hem; machine stitch close to inner fold.

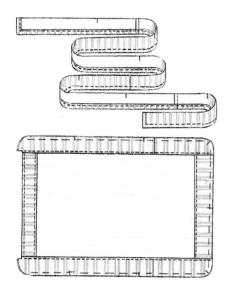

10 Sectioning skirt and top panel To ensure even gathers, divide the total length of the skirt into eight equal sections, marking the divisions on the top edge with a dressmaker's pencil. Measure all round the top panel, from one side of the hemmed top edge to the other. Divide this amount by eight and mark the sections on the top panel.

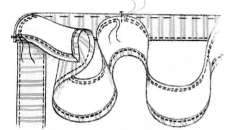

11 Gathering the skirt Work two parallel rows of gathering thread along top edge of the skirt, 6mm (¼in) and 1cm (⅜in) in from the raw edge. To make drawing up the threads easier, stop and start stitching at the section marks. Right sides together and raw edges matching, pin the skirt to the top panel, starting and ending at each end of the hemmed edge and matching the section marks.

12 Stitching the skirt Draw up gathering stitches on the skirt to fit the top panel, adjusting the gathers evenly within each section, but pulling them slightly tighter at the corners to allow extra fabric for ease. Tack and stitch the skirt in place, stitching through all the layers. Clip into the seam allowance at the corners of the skirt and unpick the tacking. Trim the seam allowances and neaten the raw edge with zigzag stitch. Press seam towards skirt.

▲ *Making curtains and a bed valance from the same fabric is the most direct route to a stylishly coordinated bedroom scheme.*

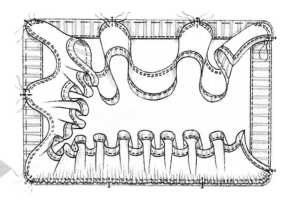

VALANCE FOR A FRAMED BED
As well as headboards, some beds have legs or footboards attached to the outside of the bed base. In this case, stitch a double hem at the ends of each skirt piece, as in step 9 above, and then attach them to the sides and foot of the base in separate sections, so that they hang around the bed frame.

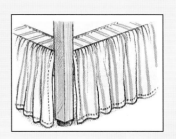

Lining the gathered skirt

Lining the skirt adds weight and body to the valance, which is useful if the main fabric is fairly lightweight. The lining is not seen, so you can use economical sheeting or lining fabric. The lining is cut narrower than the main fabric; the extra depth of the main fabric incorporates the hem allowance. When the two layers are stitched together, you can press the seam to the back of the skirt.

To make the lined version of the gathered skirt, follow the basic steps for *Making a gathered bed valance,* on the previous pages, adding the instructions for cutting out and making up the lining, as below.

1 Cutting out Measure and cut out the top panel, skirt and border sections, following steps **1-4** on page 74. *For skirt lining:* measure total width of skirt, as in step **4** on page 74. Divide this by the width of the sheeting fabric to see how many widths to cut. Cut required number of widths, by the drop **C** less 2cm (³⁄₄in).

2 Making up the top panel Follow steps **5-8** on page 74 for adding the borders and hemming the top edge of the top panel.

3 Joining the skirt widths Join all the main fabric widths to make one long strip; press seams open. Repeat with the sheeting widths for the lining.

4 Lining the skirt Lay the lining and furnishing fabric strips right sides together, aligning the lower edges. Machine stitch along this edge.

5 Finishing off the skirt Neaten and press seam open. Match top raw edges with right sides together, and stitch the side edges. Turn to right side, press along the bottom fold and tack the top edges together. Treating the two layers as one, continue making up the skirt following steps **10-12** on the previous page.

▼ *Here, the bed's valance and cover enter enthusiastically into the general spirit of fabric teamwork in this child's bedroom.*

Sheeting fabrics

Sheeting fabric isn't just for making sheets. The generous width of the fabric makes it ideal for items from valances and duvet covers to table cloths and curtains.

Sheeting fabrics are strong and closely woven, so they wear and wash well. They are also very wide, which means you can usually avoid joining the fabric across the width of a large item. The fabric is mainly used to make flat or fitted sheets, duvet covers, valances and pillowcases, but its generous width also makes it ideal for table cloths, unlined curtains and other large items where good washability is important.

Sheeting widths

The most common width of sheeting is 228cm (90in), which is suitable for making sheets and duvet covers for double beds. Widths for single and king-size beds are also available – 175cm (69in) and 278cm (109in), respectively. The sizing information is usually printed on the fabric label, together with the fibre composition and care details.

Cotton versus cotton/polyester

Sheeting is a mediumweight fabric, usually made from 100 per cent cotton or 50 per cent cotton and 50 per cent polyester. Cotton is a hardwearing, natural fibre which is non-abrasive and absorbent, while polyester, a synthetic fibre, adds easy-care properties to the finished item. Both cotton and cotton/

▲ *For a really coordinated look, sew your own bedlinen and make accessories to match. Here, the fresh plaid used for the bedspread makes attractive scatter cushions, as well as an unusual border for the pictures above the bed.*

polyester are strong and stable enough to hold their shape through repeated use and laundering, but the addition of polyester makes the fabric last longer before wearing through. Some people prefer the comfort of pure cotton bedlinen, while others like the easy-to-care-for, non-crease, non-iron benefits of a cotton/polyester blend.

Guide to sheeting fabrics

Sheeting fabrics are either dyed a solid pastel or deep colour, or printed with an attractive, colourful pattern, such as florals, stripes or checks. The following examples are typical of what is available from fabric shops and departments. Sheeting fabric is also available from some mail order fabric companies.

Plain pastel, double-bed sheeting (A) is one of the most popular fabrics for bedlinen. It is 228cm (90in) wide and made from 50 per cent cotton and 50 per cent polyester. Popular colours include pale blue, pale pink, eau de nil, lemon and cream. Plain pastel sheeting is generally less expensive to buy than deep-dye or patterned sheeting.

Plain deep-dye, double-bed sheeting (B) is 228cm (90in) wide and is made from 100 per cent cotton or an equal blend of cotton and polyester. It comes in a range of deep colours – the 100 per cent cotton sheeting producing slightly more vibrant shades.

Patterned, double-bed sheeting is 228cm (90in) wide and usually made from 50 per cent cotton and 50 per cent polyester; 100 per cent cotton sheeting is also available. It comes in a variety of designs, including **tartan (C)**, **stripes (D)**, **spots (E)** and **florals (F)**. For a more lively look, mix plain and patterned fabrics in coordinating colours – using a contrasting fabric for frills and facings, say. **Novelty patterned sheeting (G)** is much in demand for Christmas table cloths and trimmings. It is printed with gold pigment for a glittering, festive effect, and comes in a range of colours, including scarlet, green and royal blue.

Plain, king-size sheeting (H) is extra wide, at 278cm (109in), and comes in a limited range of plain colours. The sample shown here is made from 100 per cent cotton, but king-size sheeting made from 50 per cent cotton and 50 per cent polyester is also available.

Flannelette sheeting (I) is a traditional sheeting fabric, which usually comes in white only. The surface of flannelette is brushed during manufacture to give a soft, slightly fluffy nap, which looks rather like woollen flannel. This sample is 175cm (69in) wide and made from 100 per cent cotton.

Needles and stitches

- ◆ **Machine needles** Sizes 60/8 to 80/12
- ◆ **Stitch length** 1.5 to 2 millimetres (18 to 12 stitches per inch)
- ◆ **Hand needles** Betweens sizes 5 to 10
- ◆ **Thread** Cotton for cotton sheeting; polyester for cotton/polyester blends

Prewashing the fabric

Prewash 100 per cent cotton sheeting to remove any dressing from the fabric, which can cause skipped stitches. Wash and dry the fabric in the same way you will treat the finished item, then press with a hot iron on a steam setting.

Determining the right side

Before cutting out, determine which is the right side of the fabric. This is easy to work out when the fabric is printed, as the pattern is stronger on the right side. On plain coloured sheeting, run your finger along the selvedge – the fabric around the tiny holes on the selvedge is smoother on the right side.

Laying and cutting out

Sheeting fabrics are very stable in construction and do not slip, so you can lay the fabric directly on to a table or cardboard cutting board. Fold the fabric in a double layer, with the right sides together and the selvedges lined up. Smooth out the fabric, pin the layers together, then cut out as required using sharp dressmaking shears.

▶ *An unfitted white sheet draped over this single bed provides a simple and inexpensive alternative to a frilled valance – just the right look for this casually furnished child's bedroom.*

Sewing advice

When making duvet covers, investigate the types of fastenings available, such as snap-fastener tape and touch-and-close tape (Velcro). Alternatively, you could use ribbon ties or buttons and button-holes to fasten the cover.

Seams

Sheeting fabrics are easy to sew, but tend to fray when in use, unless the raw edges are neatened. Use a plain seam for straight seams, and eliminate fraying by sewing a turned and stitched or zigzag finish, or by overlocking the edges of the seam allowances. For strength and neatness, use a double-stitched seam, such as a French or flat-fell seam.

Hems

Narrow double hems work well on most bedlinen and should be secured with a neat row of machine stitching close to the fold. Wide hems at the top of flat sheets can be turned and machine stitched with the addition of decorative cording or narrow lace edging, if you

wish. The edges of informal table cloths, particularly circular and oval shapes, look good finished with contrasting coloured bias binding.

▲ *Candy-coloured, cotton gingham makes a delightful table covering at this alfresco reception. Sheeting is ideal for making table cloths, as it saves time and money. With such a wide fabric, you probably won't need any joining seams – just cut the fabric to shape and finish the edges with a plain hem or bias binding.*

Fabric care

Laundering

Treat stains as soon as they occur, and wash items before they become really soiled. Always wash deep colours separately for the first two or three washes, to avoid colour running into other items.

Cotton/polyester sheeting can be machine washed at 40°C. Spin dry it, using the shortest spin programme on your machine to minimize creasing. Take the time to smooth out any wrinkles, and fold the sheeting neatly before hanging it up to dry.

Cotton sheeting should be treated in the same way as cotton/polyester sheeting, as described, but may be washed at hotter temperatures, up to 60°C. Air the fabric thoroughly after laundering and pressing to avoid mildew forming – a mould which can rot the fibres.

Pressing

Cotton/polyester sheeting need only be pressed if it looks creased. Use a synthetic setting on your iron.

Cotton sheeting can withstand temperatures up to 210°C, so use a hot iron and plenty of steam.

Shirred bedlinen

*Make your bed the focus of attention by dressing it in frilled bedlinen
with a crisp and sophisticated finish. All it takes to bring about a stunning
transformation is a strip of sheeting fabric and colourful thread.*

The bed has pride of place in the bedroom, so it's worth dressing it in attractive bedlinen. These crisp shirred frills will give a smart and colourful finish to any plain, ready-made sheets and pillowcases – and they're easy and inexpensive to make.

The frill is embellished with rows of zigzag stitching; for a coordinated look, choose a thread colour that matches or

tones with your bedroom scheme. The shirred effect is achieved by working the stitching over lengths of extra strong thread; these threads are then drawn up to pull the fabric into gathers. This technique is rather like true shirring, which uses lengths of shirring elastic instead of thread.

It's important to work the zigzag stitching from the wrong side of the

▲ *Bright blue zigzag stitching on white bedlinen creates a clean, crisp look. This design can take on many different guises; try using threads in a mixture of colours, for example, for a rainbow effect.*

frill, with extra strong thread in a contrasting colour on the bobbin. On the finished frill, the contrasting thread will be visible on the right side.

Making shirred frills for bedlinen

The steps below explain how to add shirred frills to a flat sheet and pillowcases. For the frills, use sheeting fabric to match the bedlinen, ideally with the same composition, so their laundry requirements are the same.

For a single sheet and pillowcase, you will need 60m (66yd) of contrasting extra strong thread and 30m (33yd) of matching extra strong thread.

You will need

- ◆ Flat sheet and pillowcase(s)
- ◆ Matching sheeting fabric (see chart for amounts)
- ◆ Contrasting extra strong thread
- ◆ Matching extra strong thread
- ◆ Matching sewing thread

1 Cutting the frills Cut 16cm (6¼in) strips across the full fabric width. *For the pillow:* measure the short edge and double it. Cut one strip to this length. *For the sheet:* measure the top edge and double it. Join enough strips to make a piece this length, avoiding a central seam; use French seams or 3mm (⅛in) plain seams neatened with zigzag stitch.

2 Hemming the short ends Press a double 6mm (¼in) hem along the short ends of the frill; machine stitch, using a medium length straight stitch.

3 Zigzagging the hem Press a double 6mm (¼in) hem along one long edge. With matching ordinary thread on top and contrasting extra strong thread on the bobbin, set your machine to a medium length, medium width zigzag stitch. With the wrong side facing up, zigzag stitch the hem.

4 Starting shirring Press a 1cm (⅜in) hem on the other long edge. Cut matching extra strong thread 20cm (8in) longer than hem edge – this is the shirring thread. Place on wrong side of hem, 3mm (⅛in) from raw edge. Zigzag stitch over it, just inside the raw edge.

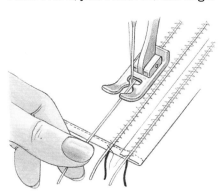

5 Finishing shirring Work five more shirring rows, as in step **4**, with presser foot edge against previous row. Pull thread ends to wrong side; knot.

▲ *A single row of zigzag stitching at the edge of the frill adds definition, while the broad band of shirring creates an appealing crumpled texture.*

6 Drawing up the threads Pull both ends of all six shirring threads to gather up the frill evenly, until it is the same length as edge of the sheet or pillowcase. Knot the shirring threads in pairs to secure them, and trim.

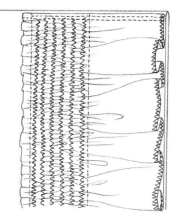

7 Attaching the frill Position the frill right side up, matching the hemmed edge to the edge of the pillowcase or sheet; pin. Stitch in place at the top and bottom of the shirred panel, then along the short ends, catching in the shirring threads.

SHEETING FABRIC AMOUNTS				
Sheeting width	*228cm*	*90in*	*278cm*	*109in*
Single sheet and 1 pillowcase	*40cm*	*½yd*	*40cm*	*½yd*
Double sheet and 2 pillowcases	*50cm*	*½yd*	*50cm*	*½yd*
King size sheet and 2 pillowcases	*70cm*	*¾yd*	*50cm*	*½yd*

Lacy bedlinen

Pure white bedlinen embellished with lace has a timeless appeal that suits many bedroom styles. Create your own by adding a lace border and frill or by trimming ready-made white bedlinen with lace.

You could spend a fortune dressing a bed with ready-made white bedlinen, beautifully embellished with white-on-white lace frills and borders. However, if you welcome the creative challenge and satisfaction of trimming or making your own, you can save yourself a huge expense.

Plain white polycotton sheets, duvets and pillowcases are widely available and inexpensive. Simply stitch on lace trimmings, in the form of mitred borders and rows of edgings, to create the luxury feel. Don't worry too much about white being an impractical colour, as polycotton is easy to wash and relatively crease-resistant.

To make your own bedlinen from scratch – and you will need to do this if you want to introduce frills – use white polycotton sheeting. It comes in 228cm (90in) widths and you can buy it from department stores. Alternatively, for a more authentic heirloom effect, use 100 per cent cotton or fine linen sheeting.

Buying lace

Lace is available with different fibre contents and it is advisable to try and match the lace to the sheeting. Pure cotton lace is the best choice for cotton sheeting, while polyester, nylon or polycotton lace can be used on polycotton sheeting. It is available with straight and shaped edges and is named as follows:

Edging lace has one straight edge and one decorative, shaped edge. Use it along the edge of a sheet or pillowcase or for gathering up into a frill.

Galloon lace is shaped on both long edges and is better set in from the edge of the bedlinen.

Border lace has two straight edges.

◄ *For the quickest results, stitch lace on to ready-made bedlinen. Here, rows of lace, stitched along the top edge of a sheet and outer edges of pillowcases, looks enticing and effective. The lace can be machined or hand stitched in place.*

Making frilled lacy bedlinen

It is easy to add a lacy frill and topstitch an impressive mitred lace border on to bedlinen if you make it yourself. To make this pretty, lace-trimmed set, you need to refer back to the instructions for making a plain and frilled duvet cover and pillowcase on pages 65–72. The steps given below explain how to stitch the mitred lace border and add in the lace frill.

You will need

- ◆ White polycotton/cotton sheeting – twice length of duvet plus 14cm (5½in)
- ◆ Border lace and edging lace, both approximately 6-8cm (2¼-3¼in) deep (see chart for amounts)
- ◆ Snap-fastener tape – 100cm (39½in) for a single bed, 150cm (59in) for a double bed and 160cm (63in) for a king size bed
- ◆ Tape measure
- ◆ Matching sewing thread
- ◆ Dressmaker's pencil

LACE AMOUNTS

The amount of lace you will need to buy will depend on the size of your duvet:

Size	Border		Edging	
	m	yd	m	yd
Single	5.2	5⅞	10.4	11¾
Double	6.5	7⅓	12	13½
King size	7.5	8½	13.6	15⅓
Pillowcase	1.3	1½	4.6	5⅛

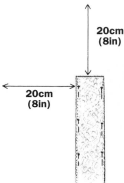

20cm (8in)

20cm (8in)

Duvet cover

1 Preparing the duvet Following steps **1-3** on page 67, cut out the duvet and stitch on the snap-fastener tape.

2 Starting the border Starting at one corner, pin border lace in place on right side with the outer edge 20cm (8in) from the edge of the duvet.

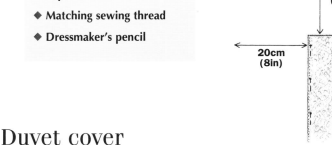

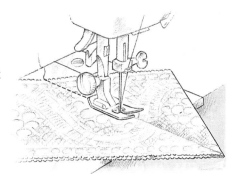

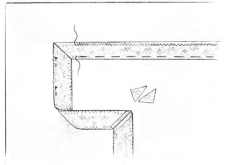

3 Forming the mitred corners At the first corner, fold the lace diagonally to form a right angle. Press and pin. Continue to pin lace in place, repeating the fold at the next two corners. At the last corner, fold lace diagonally over raw edge. Press.

4 Stitching the mitres Remove the pins at each corner and lift the lace off the duvet. On the wrong side, stitch each corner of the trim on the diagonal foldline, beginning at the inner edge.

5 Completing border Trim seam allowances of mitres to 6mm (¼in). Press seams open. Re-pin border and tack all round. Using a small, open zigzag stitch, topstitch to secure. Remove tacking and press.

◀ *For this pretty set, a soft, wide edging lace is used for the frill and a straight-edged lace for the border. On the pillowcase, the lace is mitred to form a diamond shape.*

Pillowcase

1 Cutting out Follow step **1** on page 72 for cutting out the panels. As a guide to positioning the lace border, press the pillowcase front into quarters.

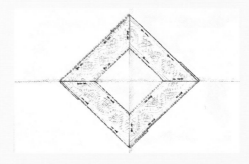

2 Adding lace border Fold the border lace into quarters. Mark with pins. Position the lace right side up on the right side of the pillowcase front, in a diamond shape, matching pins to pressed creases. Prepare the mitred corners and stitch on lace as given in steps **2-5**, left.

3 Finishing pillowcase Join the raw ends of the edging lace with French seams. Divide and mark lace into four equal sections. Attach the frill and make up the case following steps **3-5** on page 72.

6 Adding the frill Neaten the raw ends of the edging lace by turning under a narrow hem. Referring to steps **3-5** on pages 70–71, gather and tack the frill to right side of duvet, taking the lace around three sides only and dividing only three sides of the duvet into quarters. Stop the lace 6mm (¼in) from the hem stitching.

7 Assembling the duvet Position the two duvet pieces right sides together, aligning the snap fasteners without doing them up. Pin, then stitch the two sides and base of the duvet cover, taking a 1.5cm (⅜in) seam. Clip the two sides of the press fastener tape together.

Tip

PRE-FRILLED LACE EDGING
Look out for pre-frilled lace edging and use to make the frilled edgings You will need half the edging lace quantities given in the chart.

8 Completing the opening Follow step **6** on page 67 to complete the opening. Neaten seams, clip corners and turn the duvet cover right side out.

Trimming ready-made bedlinen

An easy and effective way to trim a plain sheet is to stitch rows of lace to the top edge – you can add as many rows of lace as you like. The same idea can be used for duvets and pillowcases. Add the rows of lace to the top edge of the duvet and one short edge of the pillowcase. Alternatively, add a mitred border following the steps on the previous page.

When applying lace to ready-made pillowcases you will find it easier to handstitch the lace, as it can be difficult to get the area under the machine. Use small running or overcast stitches.

As a guide to the quantities you need, refer to the sizes of sheets and pillowcase given below. Multiply the width of the sheet or pillowcase by the number of rows of lace you intend to add, and include a small extra amount for neatening the raw edges of the lace.

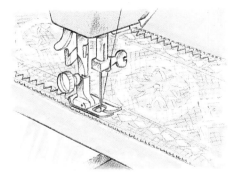

Stitching on lace by hand Cut the lace to desired length, adding 2cm (¾in) for turnings. Pin the lace in place, turning under the raw edges by 1cm (⅜in). *On border lace,* use short running stitches close to each edge, concealing the stitches in the lace. If it is very wide, you may want to work extra stitches along the centre. *On edging lace,* stitch close to the straight edge.

Stitching on lace by machine Cut the lace to desired length, adding 2cm (¾in) for turnings. Pin, then tack the lace in place, turning under the raw edges by 1cm (⅜in). Set the machine to a narrow zigzag and use matching thread. *On border lace,* stitch down each side of the lace, close to the edge. *On edging lace,* stitch close to the straight edge.

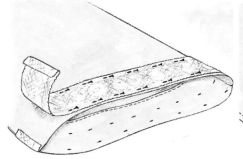

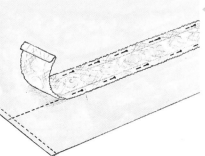

Trimming a sheet Cut each strip of lace to the width of the sheet plus 2cm (¾in) for neatening raw ends. Pin the lace to right side of the top end of sheet, folding raw ends in by 1cm (⅜in) so folded edge aligns with sheet edge. Machine or handstitch lace in place, stitching down short edges as well.

▼ *Starched pillowslips edged with cotton lace look so fresh. The top pillowcase is trimmed with a mitred border.*

Trimming a pillowcase Handstitch the lace to the front of the pillowcase, mitring the corners as given in *Duvet Cover,* steps **2-5,** on page 84. Alternatively (as shown above), start at a seam and pin the lace around the short end of the pillowcase, turning in and overlapping the raw end at the join. Handstitch it in place, taking care to stitch through one layer of the pillowcase at a time.

STANDARD BEDDING SIZES

	Length		Width	
	cm	in	cm	in
Single sheet	260	70	180	102
Double sheet	260	102	230	90
King sheet	275	108	275	108
Pillowcase	75	30	50	20

Making a bedspread

There are two main types of bedspread: the loose, throw-over cover, which is just a flat cover, and the fitted bedspread, which is seamed to fit the shape of the bed.

Throw-over covers are just single pieces of fabric, often trimmed into curves at the bottom corners for a smooth finish. They can be lined for extra body, and for extra comfort they can also be interlined and quilted. Generally, these bedcovers reach the floor, but if you have a pretty bed valance, you can make a shorter cover so that the valance will remain on show. If you need to join fabric pieces, avoid a central seam which would look obvious in the finished cover.

Fitted covers have a flat panel across the top of the bed with separate strips at the sides and base for a neat fit. The side panels can be plain or pleated at the corners for ease. For a softer look, the side panels can be gathered on to the top piece. Covered piping, between the top and side panels, will add a neat finish.

Lined throw-over cover

This is the easiest type of cover to make because you don't have to worry about getting a precise fit.

The bedcover reaches the bedhead, but if you wish to have a tuck-in to go under the pillows, add 30-40cm (12-15¾in) to the cut lengths in step **2**. Note: take 1.5cm (⅝in) seams throughout.

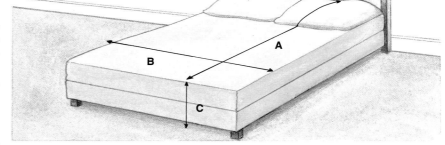

You will need

- ◆ **Fabric and lining**
- ◆ **Tape measure**
- ◆ **Dressmakers' scissors**
- ◆ **Matching threads**
- ◆ **Tailors' chalk or dressmakers' marker pen**
- ◆ **Saucer or plate to draw around**

1 Measuring up With the pillows in place, measure the length (**A**) down the centre of the bed, the width (**B**), and the depth (**C**) of the bed. Then decide whether the bedspread is to be floor-length or shorter. If you want it shorter, decide how far off the floor it should finish, and deduct this from measurement **C**. The finished bedspread will be **A** + **C** long and **B** + **C** + **C** wide.

2 Cutting out For the centre piece, cut out a full-width piece of fabric **A** + **C** long, plus 3cm (1¼in) for seams. For the sides, cut two pieces of fabric the same length as the main piece, and half the remaining width of the finished bedspread, adding 4.5cm (1⅞in) to each piece for seam allowances. Repeat to cut out the lining pieces.

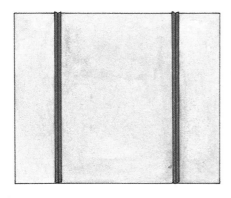

3 Joining the pieces Pin a side piece to each long edge of the centre piece, with the right sides together. Stitch the seams, then press them open. Repeat with the lining.

4 Shaping the bedspread For a neat finish, shape each lower corner of the bedspread into a curve. Just place a plate or saucer on the wrong side of the fabric at each corner and draw round it with tailors' chalk or a dressmakers' marker pen. Cut along the drawn curve. Use the main fabric as a guide for shaping the lining fabric in the same way.

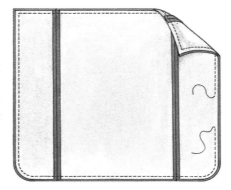

5 Attaching the lining Pin the lining and main fabrics together with the right sides facing, and stitch them together all round, leaving a 40cm (16in) gap in one side to turn through. Snip into the seam allowances at the curved corners and trim them at the angled corners, then turn the fabrics to the right side through the gap. Tuck in the seam allowances at the gap and slipstitch them. Press the bedspread.

Lined fitted cover

This type of cover has a more formal appearance than a throw-over cover. It is lined for a smart finish, and it can be interlined, too, for warmth and extra body. The side seams are piped, and it has corner pleats, both of which you can make from a contrast fabric for added detail. Arrange the pattern on the cover so that it runs vertically on each side panel and down the top piece.

You will need

- ◆ Fabric
- ◆ Contrast fabric (or main fabric) for the piping and pleats
- ◆ Lining
- ◆ Interlining (optional)
- ◆ Piping cord
- ◆ Tape measure and scissors
- ◆ Matching threads

Cutting list

Measure the bed as for *Lined throw-over cover* step 1 on page 87, and cut out the following:

From main fabric
- One rectangle for the top piece the length of the bed (A) plus 3cm (1¼in) by the width of the bed (B) plus 3cm (1¼in) – if necessary, join fabric pieces together, using a full width of fabric in the centre, with narrower pieces on each side
- Two rectangles for the side panels the length of the bed (A) plus 3cm (1¼in) by the depth of the finished bedcover (C) plus 3cm (1¼in); join fabric as necessary
- One rectangle for the base panel the width of the bed (B) plus 3cm (1¼in) by the finished depth of the bedcover (C) plus 3cm (1¼in); join fabric as necessary

From contrast or main fabric
- Two rectangles for the pleats, 50-76cm (20-30in)-wide by the depth of the cover plus 3cm (1¼in)
- Bias strips, the measurement round the piping cord plus 3cm (1¼in) wide – twice the length of the sides and base of the cover plus seams

From lining and interlining
- One piece the same size as each main fabric piece

Note: take 1.5cm (⅝in) seams throughout

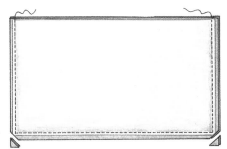

1 Preparing the panels Place the main fabric base panel on the corresponding lining piece with the right sides facing and the raw edges matching. Pin the interlining on top of the main fabric. Stitch the layers together round the sides and lower edge. Trim the interlining close to the stitching, and trim the seam allowances of all the layers at the corners. Turn the panel right sides out and press it. Tack the layers together across the top. Repeat with the two side panels and corner pleats.

2 Preparing the top piece Pin the main fabric, lining and interlining together for the top piece, as in step **1**. Stitch them together along the top short edge only, then turn them right sides out and tack the layers together around the raw edges.

3 Attaching the piping Join the bias strips to make one long piece, then wrap this round the piping cord, with the right side out. Turn in the binding at one end of the piping to neaten it, then pin it to one side of the top piece, with the neatened end at the seam. Pin it to the side and base edges, snipping into the bias fabric at the corners for ease, and finishing at the top end on the other side. Tuck in the bias fabric to neaten this end. Tack the piping in place.

4 Attaching the panels Lay out the top piece, with the main fabric up. Pin on the side and base panels, with the main fabric face down and the raw edges matching.

Find the centre of each corner pleat piece along the tacked edge and snip into the seam allowance at this point, almost up to the stitching line. Pin a corner pleat to each base corner of the bedcover, with the snipped edge at the corner. Tack the layers together.

5 Stitching the seam Adjust the tension on your sewing machine to allow for the thickness of the fabric layers, then test the tension on scraps of interlining and fabric. Stitch the layers together all round, making sure you don't catch the sides of the panels in the seam. Trim the interlining seam allowances to the stitching to reduce bulk, and trim all the seam allowances at the corners. Turn the bedspread right sides out and press it.

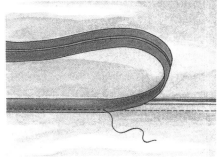

6 Neatening the seams Join the remaining bias strips to make a piece long enough to go round the sides and base of the top piece. Fold in the long raw edges by 1.5cm (⅝in) and press them. Turn under and press the raw ends. Tack the bias strip over the raw edges of the bedspread and then machine stitch it in place.

Floral bedcover

*The inviting softness of a quilted bedcover makes the
focal point of any bedroom. Even the simplest quilting
design highlights the pattern of a fabric.*

This is the first of a series of ideas on how to dress a bed completely – from eye-catching bedcover and fitted valance to padded headboard, bolster and cushions at the bed head.

You can make a lightly quilted bedcover to top a duvet, or use a thickly quilted one, teamed with a toning sheet, as an alternative to a summer duvet. The top fabric is backed with wadding and then stitched through to hold the layers together. Although quilts are traditionally stitched by hand, machine stitching is much easier and quicker.

A contrast border greatly adds to the finished look of a quilted bedcover, as you can accent one of the colours in a patterned fabric or give interest to a plainer fabric by adding a patterned border. An extra layer of wadding puffs out the border, adding emphasis and body to the edge of the quilt.

▼ *A quilt has all the traditions of an heirloom, so make it really special with some interesting details. Here, gold-splashed glass beads are stitched between the quilting and the border, drawing attention to the contrasting colours.*

Selecting suitable fabrics

Most light to mediumweight furnishing cottons are suitable for quilting. When selecting a patterned fabric, look for one which will give you an easy stitching guide – such as stripes, checks or diamonds – to avoid having to mark quilting guidelines. Alternatively, choose a fabric with an obvious pattern and outline a repeated motif. Even a small amount of quilting achieves a good effect. Use a thread which matches the main colour in the pattern for a subtle look, or choose a contrasting thread for more emphasis.

Fabric amounts

Before you start measuring up, decide how long you want your finished bedcover to be. The instructions given here are for one which covers the bed and hangs approximately 7.5cm (3in) below the bottom of the mattress, leaving the valance showing. You can adjust the measurements to make one that reaches the floor, if you prefer.

For the bedcover You'll need approximately two lengths of 120cm (48in) wide furnishing fabric for a full length quilt for a standard single or double bed. A short queen size quilt can also be cut from two lengths of fabric, while a full length queen or king size quilt requires three lengths of fabric.

For the lining You'll need the same amount of lining as furnishing fabric. It's a good idea to use polyester/cotton sheeting fabric for the lining, as you should only need one length.

For the wadding for the bedcover You'll need approximately two lengths of 96cm (38in) wide wadding for a standard single bed, and three lengths for a double, queen or king size bed. It's also possible to buy wadding in pre-packaged amounts for single, double, queen and king size beds, which avoids the need to join widths together.

Manoeuvring large amounts of fabric and wadding through a sewing machine can be difficult, so choose a lightweight wadding – about 60-100g (2-4oz) – to avoid unnecessary bulk, and place the sewing machine on a large work surface to help support the weight of the quilt.

For the border The instructions here are for a 5cm (2in) wide border, added to the sides and bottom edge of the cover – the top edge is left plain as it is tucked behind the pillows. The fabric for the border is cut on the bias. Allow 1.5m (1⅔yd) for a single quilt and 2m (2yd) for a double. You can cut all the strips of wadding for the border from half a full length, butting the lengths together.

Joining fabric widths

If you need to join fabric widths, use one full width of fabric and add strips on either side to make up the required width. To join wadding, butt the two edges together and work large oversewing stitches across the join.

Making the quilted bedcover

You will need

- ◆ Furnishing fabric
- ◆ Contrast fabric for border
- ◆ Wadding
- ◆ Lining fabric (sheeting)
- ◆ Matching thread
- ◆ Tape measure
- ◆ Pins, needle
- ◆ Safety pins
- ◆ Dressmaker's pencil
- ◆ Even-feed machine foot
- ◆ Small glass beads

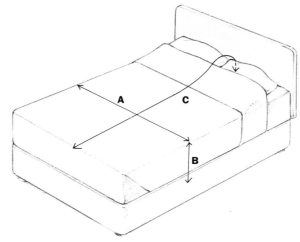

1 Measuring up With your usual bedlinen in place, measure the width of the bed (**A**) and the required drop less 5cm (2in) for the border (**B**). Measure the length (**C**) from behind the pillow to the foot of the bed. Add 30cm (12in) to length if you want to tuck bedcover neatly under the pillow.

2 Working out the size *For the width:* add twice **B** to **A**. *For the length:* add **B** to **C**, plus the pillow allowance if required. Add 15cm (6in) to width and length for seams and hems and to compensate for shrinkage caused by the quilting.

3 Cutting out Allowing for pattern matching, cut enough lengths of fabric to make up the required width. Repeat for wadding and lining. Join fabric widths as necessary, right sides together, and press the seams open. Join the wadding pieces and lay the fabric on top of the wadding, right side up.

◄ This close-up of the bedcover shows how the quilting has been used to pick out and highlight parts of the design. You don't need to stitch around every single flower to create an effective look – for the best results, decide which areas you want to emphasize and stitch each motif in the same way.

5 **Preparing to quilt** Attach an even-feed sewing machine foot and experiment on a scrap of fabric and wadding to get the best stitch length and tension. Roll sides of the quilt tightly towards the centre, securing them in place with safety pins, and leaving a flat working area of about 50cm (20in) down the centre.

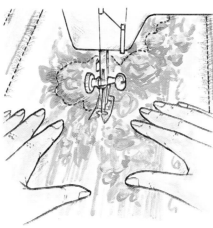

6 **Quilting the fabric** Start stitching in the centre of the quilt and work outwards to one side. Always stitch parallel lines in the same direction. Gradually unroll the quilt as you work, rolling it up on the other side. When outlining a motif, move the whole quilt under the needle to change direction. To turn a corner, leave the needle in, raise the foot and pivot the quilt.

4 **Tacking the layers together** Working from the centre outwards, pin, then tack, through the fabric and wadding, diagonally from corner to corner and 1cm (³⁄₈in) in from each edge. Select the pattern lines to be quilted and tack roughly along these.

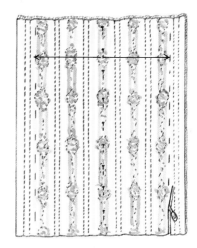

7 **Trimming the width** When the quilting is complete, fold the bedcover down the centre, mark the fold with a line of pins and then lay it out flat. From the centre line, measure half the finished width on each side less 5cm (2in) for border, plus 1.5cm (⁵⁄₈in) for seam allowance. Mark with a dressmaker's pencil, then repeat at 30cm (12in) intervals along length of quilt. Cut along the marked lines.

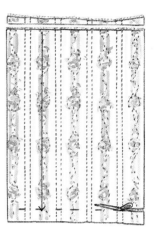

8 **Trimming the length** Trim the top edge to a straight line. Measure the finished length, less 5cm (2in) for the border, plus 1.5cm (⁵⁄₈in) for the seam allowance. Mark and repeat at intervals across the width as in step **7**, above. Cut along the marked line.

Tip

USING READY-QUILTED FABRICS
If you don't want to quilt your own pattern, look out for ready-quilted fabrics, which are available from some larger fabric departments – all you need to do is add the lining and edging.

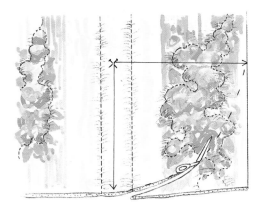

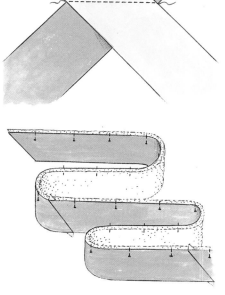

9 **Rounding the corners** At each bottom corner of the quilt, measure **B** plus a 1.5cm (⅝in) seam allowance in from the side and bottom edges; mark the point where they cross with a pin. From the pin, measure the same amount at 5cm (2in) intervals all round the corner, then join the marks to make a curve. Cut along the marked curve.

▼ *Individual glass beads, splashed with gold, add a colourful touch and textural interest around the border.*

10 **Adding the lining** Right sides together, lay bedcover on lining and trim lining to fit. Pin and stitch along top edge only. Turn lining to wrong side and trim corner curves. Pin and tack the layers together around remaining raw edges.

11 **Cutting out the border** From border fabric, cut enough bias strips, 13cm (5¼in) wide, to go around sides and bottom of the quilt, plus 10cm (4in). Allow enough fabric for a few tiny pleats to form around curved corners. Repeat in wadding.

12 **Making up the border** Join the bias strips together and press the seams open. Join the wadding strips by butting them together and oversewing. Then, right side up, pin the fabric to the wadding.

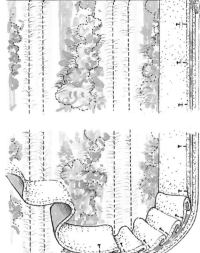

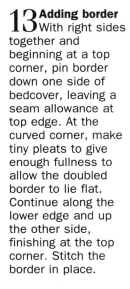

13 **Adding border** With right sides together and beginning at a top corner, pin border down one side of bedcover, leaving a seam allowance at top edge. At the curved corner, make tiny pleats to give enough fullness to allow the doubled border to lie flat. Continue along the lower edge and up the other side, finishing at the top corner. Stitch the border in place.

14 **Finishing off** Roll raw edge of border to back. Turn in seam allowance to meet stitching line; pin all round, making tiny pleats at corners to match those on right side. Turn in ends of border level with top edge. Slipstitch all round. Stitch glass beads along stitching between quilting and border.

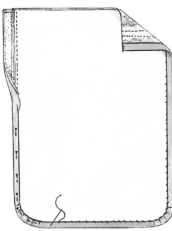

Floral valance

*A softly tailored, quilted bed valance is the perfect foil for a
beautiful quilted bedcover. Choose a coordinating fabric with a
design that has its own built-in quilting guidelines.*

With its simple lines, this style of valance is an elegant way to hide the base and legs of the bed, as well as any unsightly items you have stored underneath. It fills the gap between quilt and floor, without stealing the limelight from a beautiful bedcover.

A fitted valance is similar to a frilled valance – the skirt is sewn to a top panel that lies between the base of the bed and the mattress. However, because the skirt lies flat, it uses much less of your main fabric and provides a smoother line.

The skirt is made from a strip of lined fabric, with wadding placed between the fabric layers to give body. Choose a firmly woven, medium to lightweight furnishing fabric. Ideally, it should have a design incorporating evenly spaced straight lines, such as diamonds, checks or stripes. You can then use these lines as easy-to-follow guides when you are working your quilting. For both the

▲ *The simple lines of this valance
are designed to show off the sumptuous
quilted design, which beautifully
enhances a quilted bedcover or
dresses up a plain coloured blanket.*

skirt lining and the top panel, use poly-cotton sheeting – it is extra wide, so you won't have to join widths.

Making a fitted quilted valance

In most quilting projects, the quilting is worked before the lining is attached. However, this valance skirt is quilted with the lining in place to give a close, flat finish.

The skirt is made up from panels cut across the width of the fabric. This makes it easier to match the pattern on the fabric, and it is an economical way to use the most costly element of your project. You will need four to five panels, depending on the width of both the fabric and the bed.

Because the quilting makes the fabric 'shrink', the skirt is cut 10cm (4in) larger than the actual measurements, and then trimmed to size after quilting.

Before measuring up, remove the mattress so that you can measure the base accurately. An extra allowance is built into the skirt width, so that it wraps around the top of the bed for a neat and secure finish.

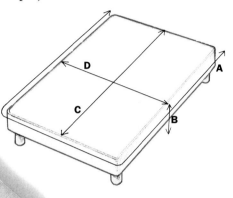

You will need

- ◆ 1.75-2.5m (1⁷⁄₈-2³⁄₄yd) of furnishing fabric for skirt
- ◆ Lightweight wadding
- ◆ 1.8-3m (2-3¹⁄₄yd) polycotton sheeting for the lining and top panel
- ◆ Matching thread
- ◆ Tape measure
- ◆ Pins and safety pins
- ◆ Even-feed machine foot
- ◆ Saucer
- ◆ Dressmaker's pencil

1 Measuring up *For the skirt width:* measure round the sides and foot end of the base (**A**). *For the skirt depth:* measure the drop from the top of the bed base to just above the floor (**B**). *For the top panel:* measure the length of the bed base (**C**) and the width (**D**).

2 Cutting out the skirt Add 37cm (14⁵⁄₈in) to **A** and 13cm (5¹⁄₈in) to **B**. Allowing for joins and pattern matching, cut enough widths of fabric to make up a long strip to this size. Repeat for both the lining and the wadding. For the top panel, add 4.5cm (1³⁄₄in) to the length **C** and 3cm (1¹⁄₄in) to the width **D**, and cut a piece of lining to this size.

3 Preparing the skirt With right sides together, and matching the pattern, join the skirt panels to make one long strip. Press the seams open. Repeat for the lining. Join the wadding panels, as required, by butting them together and oversewing.

▶ Choose a simple fabric design, preferably with straight lines which you can use as a stitching guide when quilting – this harlequin fabric in rich tones is ideal.

4 Making up the skirt Lay the fabric right side up on the wadding. Lay the lining on top, right side down. Pin and stitch along the lower and side edges through all three layers. Trim the corners, turn the lining out to the back and press.

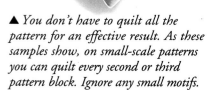

▲ You don't have to quilt all the pattern for an effective result. As these samples show, on small-scale patterns you can quilt every second or third pattern block. Ignore any small motifs.

5 Tacking the layers Starting in the centre and working outwards, tack the layers together in lines about 30cm (12in) apart, and along the top edge. Decide which pattern lines you want to quilt and tack roughly along them.

6 Quilting the skirt Using the even-feed sewing machine foot, check your stitch length and tension on a scrap of fabric, wadding and lining. Then work the quilting on the skirt, as for the quilted bedcover, steps **5-6** on page 91.

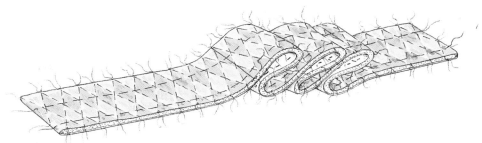

7 Trimming to length When the quilting is complete, measure the desired skirt length plus 1.5cm (⅝in) for the seam allowance. Trim excess from the top edge.

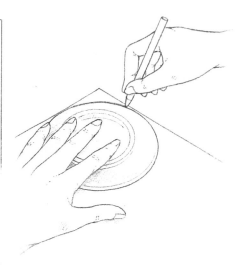

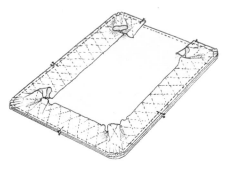

8 **Hemming the top panel** On one short end of the top panel, measure and mark 12cm (4¾in) in from each corner. Using sharp scissors, make a 3cm (1¼in) long snip at right angles to the raw edge at the marked point. Between the snips, press under a double 1.5cm (⅝in) hem and stitch close to the fold.

▼ *The quilting lines on this fitted valance enhance the bold checked design. The quilting was easy to work by using the checked lines as guides.*

9 **Rounding the corners** Place the saucer upside down on one corner at the foot of the top panel. Carefully align the rim of the saucer with the raw edges of the fabric. Using the dressmaker's pencil, draw round the saucer to curve the corner, then cut along the line. Curve the remaining three corners in the same way.

10 **Assembling the valance** Measure round the top panel from each end of the hemmed section, divide into four and mark with pins. Divide the skirt lengthways into four sections and mark with pins along the top edge. With right sides together and matching raw edges and pins, pin the skirt to top panel, easing it round the corners, then stitch.

11 **Finishing off** Clip the corners. trim the seam allowances and neaten the raw edges with zigzag stitch or by oversewing them.

Floral bedhead cushion

*A comfortable cushion hung on a pole is a stylish
and practical alternative to a conventional bedhead. It's easier
to make and you can remove the cover for regular cleaning.*

This smart bedhead cushion gives comfortable support when you are sitting up in bed, while the neat shape, smart contrasting straps and stylish pole combine to make a really eye-catching feature.

For a double bed, you can make either one large cushion or two smaller ones. You can also adapt this idea to suit a teenager's bedroom or a bedsit, where the bed is used as a sitting area during the day. Simply move the bed into a corner and hang a cushion on each wall to create a comfortable sofa.

Choose a pole that complements the mood of the room, and finish the ends with decorative finials. Make sure the pole is strong enough to take the weight of the cushion, plus some extra strain when you lean back against it. It should be roughly the width of the bed or slightly longer.

Fixing the pole

Decide how high to place the cushion (see *Buying the foam,* below) before fixing the pole to the wall. Remember to allow extra height to give room for the ties. Position the side brackets level with the sides of the bed, and add a centre bracket to help spread the load.

Buying the foam

For the pad, buy 7.5cm (3in) thick, flame resistant, medium density foam from a professional supplier who will cut it to size for you. The pad should be a little shorter than the full width of the bed, but high enough to create a comfortable back and headrest when you are sitting up. As a guide, the cushion headrest shown on the left is 7.5cm (3in) thick, 130cm (51in) wide and 56cm (22in) high.

◄ *Make the cushion cover from a closely woven fabric that coordinates with your existing bed furnishings. Choose a bold contrasting colour for the straps, which are cut extra wide for strength.*

Making the cushion bedhead

The cushion pad itself is a foam squab wrapped in wadding to give a softer, plumper shape and a more professional finish. The cover is made from two pieces of fabric. After stitching them together, a tuck is taken at each corner – this technique creates depth, allowing the cover to fit neatly round the pad. The straps are sewn on before the cover is assembled, giving plenty of support.

You will need

◆ **Foam squab**

◆ **Main fabric**

◆ **Contrast fabric**

◆ **Mediumweight wadding**

◆ **Zip, about two-thirds the width of the cushion**

◆ **Matching threads**

◆ **Tape measure**

◆ **Pins**

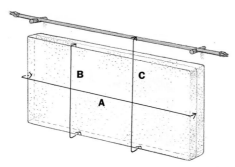

1 Measuring up Mark a line all round the foam dividing the thickness in half. *For the width:* measure from the line on one side, across the width, to the line on the other side (**A**). *For the height:* measure from the top line to the bottom line (**B**). *For the straps:* hold the pad on the wall at the desired height and measure from the top of the pole to the bottom line (**C**).

2 Cutting out *For the front and back:* add 3cm (1¼in) to **A** and **B** and cut two pieces of fabric to these measurements. *For the strap length:* double **C** and add 3cm (1¼in). Cut two fabric strips this length by 17cm (6¾in) wide.

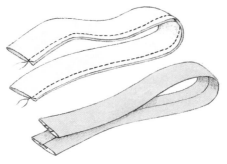

3 Making the straps With right sides and raw edges together, fold each strap in half lengthways. Pin and stitch the long edge, taking a 1cm (⅜in) seam allowance. Press the seams open, turn out and press flat with the seam centred.

4 Marking zip position Lay out the front and back cover pieces, right sides up. Centre the zip on the bottom edge and use pins on each piece to mark the points where the teeth end.

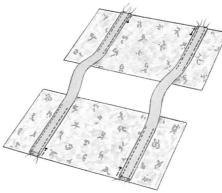

5 Stitching the straps On the right side and matching the raw edges, pin the straps, seam down, outside the marked zip ends, so that the straps run across the width of the cushion pieces. Topstitch the sides of the straps, stopping 10cm (4in) from the top raw edge of the cover pieces.

6 Stitching the seams Right sides and raw edges together, pin, then stitch the back to the front, leaving the space between the straps on the bottom edge open for the zip.

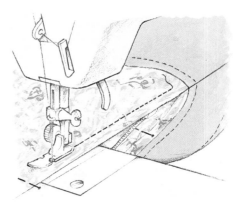

7 Inserting the zip Press the seam allowances under. With the zip closed, position the zip tape under one seam allowance, with the fold centred over the teeth, and pin. Open the zip and position and pin the other side in the same way. Topstitch both sides 1cm (⅜in) from the fold.

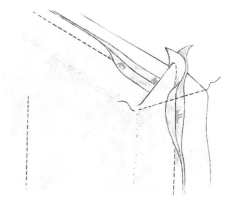

8 Squaring the corners Turn the cover wrong side out. Open out the seam allowances at one corner and bring the seams on either side of the corner together. From the point, measure half the cushion thickness down the seam, and stitch across at right angles to the seams. Repeat at the other corners.

9 Completing the cushion Lay the foam on the wadding and wrap it like a parcel, cutting the wadding to fit and folding neatly at the ends. Secure with large oversewing stitches. To fit the foam in the cover, roll or fold it to the zip width, slip it through the zip opening and open out carefully inside.

Floral cushions

*Give your bedroom an air of sumptuous comfort and romance
with a set of luxury cushions. The bolster, pillow sham and cushion
perfectly complement your quilt, valance and bedhead.*

This inviting mixture of soft cushions will give your bed a thoroughly well-dressed look, adding the final touch to the completed floral bedlinen set, with its quilted bedcover, matching fitted valance and stylish padded cushion head rest.

The cushions include a bolster, which makes a useful back and neck support when reading in bed, and a pillow sham, which is designed to turn an ordinary pillow into a cushion for daytime use. Finally, add detail with a mitred and piped cushion, and eye-catching trimmings on all three for extra colour and finish.

▲ *This luxurious set of cushions for your bed mixes styles and shapes, creating a soft, inviting pile to sink into at the end of a hard day.*

▶ *Piping and tassels are stylish trims for the mitred border cushion. Handstitch a tassel to each corner.*

Making the bolster

This bolster cover is very easy to make. It is simply a long cylinder of fabric, with the ends faced in contrasting fabric and gathered up with rope. The cover is cut longer than the bolster to make a fabric rosette at each end, which is turned out to display a contrasting facing.

Ideally, the length of the bolster should be almost the width of the bed; the one shown opposite is 23cm (9in) in diameter, which makes a comfortable neck roll. For firm support, use a foam pad, or have a fibrefill or Dacron pad made to your chosen dimensions by a soft furnishing company or cushion manufacturer. As an inexpensive and softer alternative, buy a long strip of wadding and roll it tightly to the diameter you want, and oversew the ends; cover with lining or calico.

You will need

- ◆ **Furnishing fabric**
- ◆ **Contrasting fabric for end facings**
- ◆ **2m (2¼yd) cord for ties**
- ◆ **Matching thread**
- ◆ **Bolster pad**
- ◆ **Tape measure**
- ◆ **Large safety pin**
- ◆ **Dressmaker's pencil**
- ◆ **Scissors, pins**

▶ *For the main part of the bolster, choose one of the fabrics that you used to make the bedcover or valance in your bed set. Set it off by using a plain contrast fabric for the lining, to enhance the attractive rosette of gathered fabric at each end.*

1 Measuring up At each end of the pad, mark a line across the widest point in two different directions. Where they cross is the centre. *For the length,* measure from the centre of one pad end to the other (**A**). *For the circumference,* measure all round the bolster (**B**).

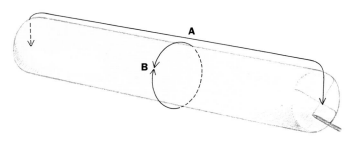

2 Cutting out the cover *For the width,* add 16cm (6⅜in) to each end of **A**. *For the length,* add 3cm (1¼in) to **B**. *For the cover,* cut one piece of your main fabric to this size; if necessary, join strips on to a width to make up the desired measurement. *For the facings,* cut two pieces of contrasting fabric 18.5cm (7⅜in) wide by the length of the cover piece.

Tip

STITCHING THE CASINGS Remove the stitching platform from your sewing machine to make stitching round the casings at end of the bolster easier.

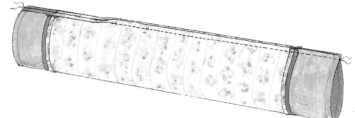

3 Adding the facings On one long edge of both facing pieces, press under 1.5cm (⅝in). Right sides together, pin the other long edge of one facing piece to each end of the main cover piece. Stitch, then press seams open.

4 Stitching the main seam Right sides together, bring the two long raw edges of the cover together, opening out the pressed edges of the facings. Pin and stitch, then press the seam open.

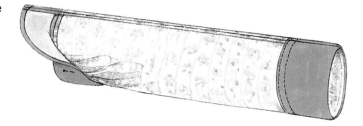

5 Stitching the casings Turn in the pressed edges of the facings. With the cover wrong side out, turn the facings to the wrong side, and pin to hold in place. Stitch close to the folded edge of the facings, then again 2.5cm (1in) in from the first stitching line; these rows form the casing.

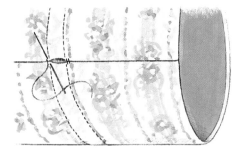

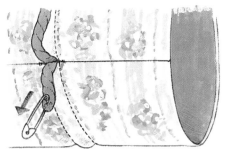

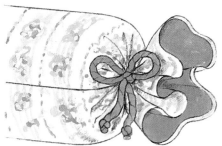

6 Making the casing holes Turn the cover out to the right side and unpick the main seam between the two rows of stitching for the casing. Neaten with a few hand stitches.

7 Inserting the cord Cut the cord in two and fasten a safety pin to one end of the first piece Thread the cord through the gap, along the casing and out again. Repeat with the other end.

8 Finishing off Knot the ends of the cord to neaten them. Insert the pad, pull up the cord tightly at each end and tie into bows. Roll back the facings to show the contrasting fabric.

Making the pillow sham

Use this pillow sham to cover a spare pillow, converting it into a decorative cushion for daytime use. You can use small fabric remnants to make the sham, as it simply consists of three strips of fabric stitched together. If you have strips of quilted fabric left over from making the quilt, you could use these – they will add an interesting dimension to the look. To finish the ends, choose a short fringe or a pretty bobble trim in a coordinating colour.

These instructions are for a pillow measuring 70 x 45cm (27½ x 17¾in).

You will need

- ◆ **Furnishing fabric for centre section**
- ◆ **Contrasting fabric for side sections**
- ◆ **1m (1⅛yd) trimming**
- ◆ **Matching thread**
- ◆ **Tape measure**

1 Cutting out the fabrics *For the centre section,* cut one rectangle of fabric 93 x 36cm (36¾ x 14¼in). *For the two end sections,* cut one rectangle 93 x 21.5cm (36¾ x 8½in), and a second rectangle 93 x 33.5cm (36¾ x 13¼in).

2 Stitching together Right sides together, pin and stitch the end sections on either side of the centre section. Trim the seam allowances to 6mm (¼in) and zigzag stitch to neaten. Press the seams open.

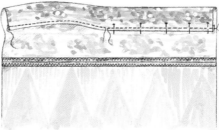

3 Stitching the flap On wider side section, press under a double 1cm (⅜in) hem on long raw edge; stitch along half of the total length only. Press under 10cm (4in) to wrong side; pin and stitch down other half of hem.

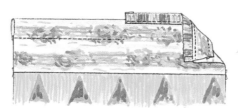

4 Trimming the flap end Cut the trim in two. On the right side, lay the trim along the outer folded edge, on the open flap section. Turn in the trim ends to neaten and topstitch in place.

5 Finishing the seams Fold the sham in half, right sides together. Stitch along the raw edges, leaving the trimmed edge open. Trim and neaten the seam allowances.

6 Completing the sham Turn the sham out to the right side and topstitch the trim neatly along the stitched end of the sham, turning in the ends at each edge to neaten.

Contemporary bedspread

The cool, classic look of this bed set is achieved with simple, inexpensive fabrics, neatly tailored to fit the bed. Decorative details are kept to a minimum for a clean, restful effect.

Whilst duvets are the optimum in convenience and comfort, it's never easy to achieve a really neat and tidy look, however many times you tug at it! The clean-cut lines of a fitted bedspread are much easier on the eye, especially if the room is dual-purpose – perhaps a study bedroom – or the bed is a daybed. The bedspread is fully lined, so in warm climates or on hot summer nights it may be substan-tial enough on its own, with just a sheet underneath, rather than a thick duvet.

The boxy shape of the bedspread, with its smart inverted pleats and contrast piping and border, is echoed by another clever cover-up: by day the pillows turn into elegant cushions, with piped and bordered pillow shams.

The set pictured here uses a simple blue and white ticking as the basis for the ensemble, and plays with assorted checks and a richly woven design in the other items. For a teenager's room, you could choose tough denim contrasted with scarlet and mixed Madras checks. Or, for a sophisticated, elegant air, go for stark white or cream woven patterns, set against classic black and white ticking, with any details picked out in black.

The smart inverted pleats, positioned at each corner and in the centre of the foot and sides, are a distinctive feature of this bedspread.

Making the fitted bedspread

The top and skirt of the bedspread are cut as separate sections and joined at the edge, in a similar way to making a bed valance. For extra impact, the seam where the two sections meet is defined by piping covered in contrasting fabric. The skirt is bound in the same contrasting fabric and features inverted pleats at each corner, and also in the centre of the side and foot sections.

The bedspread is cut long enough to tuck in at the head of the bed, but not to cover the pillows – if required, add an extra 30cm (12in) to the overall length of the bedspread.

Fabric quantities

Use the *Size chart* at the bottom of this page as a guide to buying fabric. The quantities are based on 140cm (55in) wide fabric – for narrower fabrics, you need to increase the amounts. For beds wider than a double, you need to join strips either side of a width to make up the size. Polycotton sheeting is useful for lining, as it is very wide and also washable. If you want your bedspread to be washable, check the suitability of fabrics before you buy them. You also need enough piping cord to go round the sides and foot end of the bed.

You will need

- ◆ Fabric
- ◆ Contrasting fabric
- ◆ Sheeting for lining
- ◆ Piping cord
- ◆ Matching thread
- ◆ Tape measure
- ◆ Dinner plate

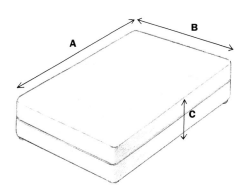

1 Measuring up With the usual bedlinen in place, measure the length of the bed from the head to the foot (**A**) and the width (**B**). Then measure the height from the top of the bed to just above the floor (**C**).

2 Cutting the top panel Add 23cm (9¼in) to **A** and 3cm (1¼in) to **B** and cut one piece from both fabric and lining to this size. If necessary, cut two lengths and join panels on either side of the central one.

3 Calculating the skirt *For the length*, double the bed length **A** and add the width **B**; then add 150cm (60in) for pleats and 3cm (1¼in) for seam allowances. *For the depth*, take 2cm (¾in) from total height **C**.

4 Cutting out the skirt Cut enough widths across the fabric to the required depth to make up the total skirt panel length after joining. (On plain fabrics you can cut along the length of the fabric.) Repeat to cut out the skirt lining.

5 Shaping the corners Join the pieces for the top panel, if necessary, and press the seams open. At the foot corners, use the plate as a template to round off the corners.

▶ *Choose a plain, toning colour for the binding to emphasize the simple lines of the bedcover, with its neatly pleated corners.*

6 Piping the top edge Make up enough piping, using the piping cord and contrasting fabric, to go round the sides and foot end of the top panel. Apply piping to top panel, clipping at the curved corners.

7 Cutting out binding Cut enough 13cm (5¼in) wide strips of contrasting fabric, on the straight of the grain, to go all around the bottom of the skirt. Join the strips together and press the seams open.

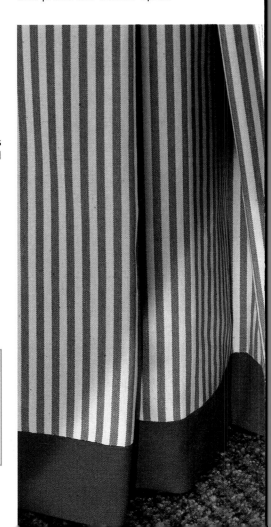

SIZE CHART							
Bed size	**Main fabric**		**Contrasting fabric**		**Sheeting**		
	m	yd	*m*	yd	*m*	yd	
Single	5	5½	1.5	1⅝	3	3⅓	
Double	6	6½	2	2¼	4	4⅜	
Queen	8.3	9	2	2¼	4	4⅜	

8 Making up the skirt Join all the fabric strips and press the seams open. Join all the lining strips in the same way. With right sides together, pin and stitch the binding along the bottom edge of the skirt; then join the lining, with right sides together, to the lower edge of the binding.

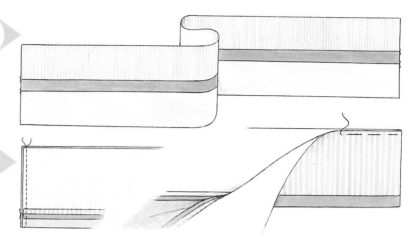

9 Stitching the sides Fold the long edges with right sides and raw edges together. Pin, then stitch, side edges together. Trim seam allowances and turn out to right side. Tack the layers together along the top edge.

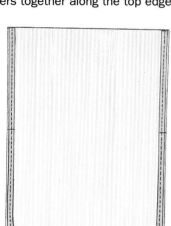

10 Marking the pleats Along the edge of the top panel, mark the corners at the foot end, and then measure and mark the centres of the foot edge and the sides.

11 Positioning the pleats Fold the skirt in half lengthways, right sides together; pin 15cm (6in) from centre fold for centre foot pleat. On each side, measure the same distance as on top panel edge from centre foot to corner mark, and make another pleat. Measure again from corner mark to centre side; make another pleat.

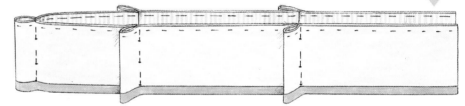

12 Forming the pleats Check the measurements and adjust the pleats if necessary. Form box pleats by flattening each pleat with the centre fold on the mark, keeping all raw edges level; tack across the top. Secure pleats in place with large cross-stitch tacking at intervals down the centre of each one, and press.

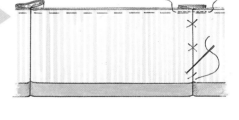

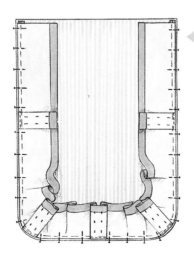

13 Attaching the skirt Right sides and raw edges together, and matching centres of pleats to marks, pin the skirt to the top panel. At top end, the skirt should finish 1.5cm (⅝in) from the raw edge of the top panel. Stitch along the tacked line through all layers, keeping the pleats flat.

14 Attaching the lining Lay the lining, right sides together, on the top panel, with the skirt smoothed down and sandwiched between. Matching raw edges, pin lining to top panel along all sides, leaving a 20cm (8in) gap at the foot end. Stitch.

15 Completing the cover Turn the cover out through the gap; slipstitch closed and press to finish. Finally, unpick the cross-tacks.

Making the pillow shams

To turn pillows into smart daytime accessories, slip them into tailored covers to match the bedcover. Crisp, flat borders and neatly piped edges give them a sophisticated air, and the bedcover lies beautifully flat beneath.

You will need

For one standard pillow:

◆ 1.2m (1³⁄₈yd) fabric

◆ Contrasting piping fabric – approximately 1m (1¹⁄₈yd)

◆ 3m (3¹⁄₄yd) piping cord

◆ Matching thread

◆ Pins

◆ Scissors

1 Cutting out *For the front:* cut one piece 83cm (32³⁄₄in) wide by 58cm (23in) deep. *For the back:* cut one piece 97cm (38¹⁄₄in) wide by 58cm (23in) deep.

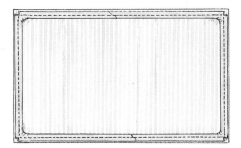

2 Adding the piping Cut bias strips from contrasting fabric and make up the piping. Using a piping or zip foot, apply the piping all round the front piece, overlapping to join the ends.

3 Hemming the back sections Fold the back piece in half lengthways and cut along the fold. On each piece, press a double 1cm (³⁄₈in) hem along the cut edge, and stitch.

4 Joining front and backs With right sides together and matching the raw edges, lay the two back sections on top of the front section, so that the hemmed edges overlap by 5cm (2in). Pin and stitch all round along the previous stitchline.

▲ *Flat borders and contrast piping give a smart, tailored finish to these simple pillow shams, complementing the bedcover beautifully.*

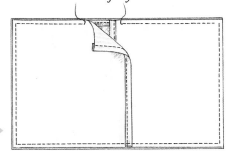

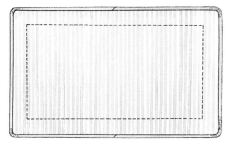

5 Finishing off Turn the cover to the right side and press. Pin and stitch all round, 5cm (2in) in from the piped edge. Finally, insert the pillow.

Contemporary bedhead cover

A removable cover for a bedhead is practicality itself – you can match a new colour scheme without complicated upholstery and, by using washable fabrics, you can keep it looking as fresh as a daisy.

This crisply detailed cover, with its neatly buttoned borders, has an elegant tailored look, ideal for cool, contemporary bedrooms. Wrap it over an existing bedhead, or make an economical chipboard base: the cover has built-in padding and simply presses together at the sides with Velcro spots.

The edges extend beyond the headboard by the width of the border on each side. The cover is cut the same front and back, so you can turn it round for even more wear (add buttons on the back as well if you want to do this). Adding borders at the sides means that for most bed sizes you can get away with one width of fabric – and, for a more economical option, you can use plain fabric offcuts for the borders. Decorate the borders with fun novelty buttons, or make covered ones for a tailored look.

▲ *Simplicity wins through in the bedroom with a wrap-over, press-together headboard cover.*

Making the cover

To work out how much fabric to buy, double the headboard depth and add 10cm (4in). You need the same amount of mediumweight wadding and lining. Allow extra for beds wider than 137cm (4ft 6in). Polycotton sheeting or any other washable cotton is suitable for the lining. Most haberdashery departments sell packets of Velcro circles, or 'spots'.

You will need

- ◆ **Furnishing fabric**
- ◆ **Contrasting fabric for borders**
- ◆ **Lining fabric**
- ◆ **Matching thread**
- ◆ **Mediumweight wadding**
- ◆ **Ten buttons**
- ◆ **Ten Sew 'n' Sew Velcro spots**
- ◆ **Tape measure, scissors**
- ◆ **Needle and pins**
- ◆ **Dressmaker's pencil**

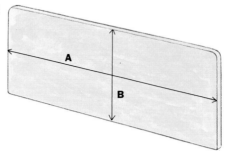

1 Cutting out Measure width (**A**) and depth (**B**) of headboard. *From fabric and lining:* cut one piece **A** plus 3cm (1¼in) by twice **B** plus 5cm (2in). *For border,* cut two pieces 13cm (5¼in) by fabric length. *From wadding:* cut a piece same length as fabric, but 10cm (4in) wider; join widths as necessary.

2 Joining pieces Right sides together, stitch a border to each side of the fabric piece. Right sides together, join the other raw edge of each border to the sides of the lining, making a tube. Press seams open.

◀ *Simple, pared down details capture the sleek, streamlined look of a modern bedroom.*

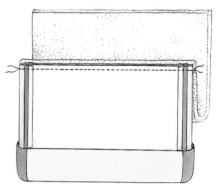

3 Adding the wadding With the border seams matching, right sides together, lay the cover on top of the wadding; stitch across the top through all layers. Turn the fabric to the right side to enclose the wadding.

4 Finishing lower edge Trim 1.5cm (⅝in) from the bottom of the wadding. Press under the seam allowances on the lower edge of cover, enclosing wadding; pin through all layers, matching seams. Topstitch along the edge, 6mm (¼in) in.

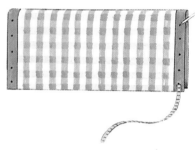

5 Positioning buttons Fold cover in two across its length. On the front half, mark the lowest button position, 5cm (2in) up from the bottom edge, on each border. Measure from this point to the top fold, divide by five and mark the other button positions.

6 Marking the Velcro positions At each button mark, push a pin through all the layers from front to back, and another from back to front at the same point. Pull the front and back apart, leaving the pins in place.

7 Adding spots On the *inside* of the *front* section, stitch a soft Velcro circle at each pin position, slipstitching round the edge to secure. Then, on the *inside* of the *back* section, stitch the corresponding hard Velcro spots at each pin.

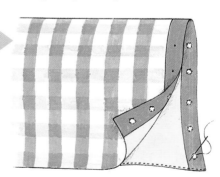

8 Adding the buttons On the *outside* of the *front*, stitch a button at each original mark, stitching through to the Velcro for a quilted effect.

Contemporary throw

Warm and cosy, this throw, with its decorative edging and neat buttoning, is as versatile as it is beautiful. It's perfect as a casual bedcover, but smart enough to dress up your sofa too.

Not quite a bedcover, and more than a blanket, a throw is one of those things that makes a house a home. Warm, welcoming and attractive to look at, this throw adds as much character to a bedroom as a patchwork quilt and is equally at home in a contemporary sitting room.

The throw is simply constructed from three fabrics. The square centre panel is surrounded by four strips of a contrast stripe, reminiscent of log cabin patchwork. Choose a floral or intricate woven design for the centre panel, and another contrasting fabric for the backing – a toning check is used here.

Subtle details make all the difference: creamy cotton fan fringing, and big buttons which match the headboard cover to hold the layers together.

▼ *The strong patterns in the throw complement the plainer bedcover and headboard, and bring the total scheme to life.*

Making the throw

The completed throw is 180cm (71in) square. However, you could easily make it larger by simply increasing the width of the border strips. A layer of light-weight wadding inside adds warmth and gives a luxurious, padded feel.

▶ *Large buttons secure the layers of the throw and add a decorative touch. For a reversible throw, stitch buttons on the underside as well.*

You will need

- ◆ **1.15m (1¼yd) of fabric for the centre panel**
- ◆ **2m (2⅛yd) of fabric for the side panels**
- ◆ **4m (4¼yd) of fabric for the backing**
- ◆ **4m (4¼yd) of lightweight wadding**
- ◆ **7.5m (8⅛yd) trim**
- ◆ **Five buttons**
- ◆ **Matching thread**

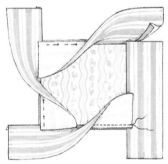

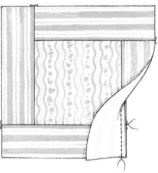

1 Cutting out *For the centre panel:* cut a 103cm (40½in) square of fabric. *For the side panels:* cut four pieces 183 x 43cm (72 x 17in). *From wadding and backing fabric:* cut two pieces 183cm (72in) long.

2 Joining side panels Right sides together and working around centre square, pin one panel to each side of square so that the short end of panel on the left lines up with the side of the square. The right end of each panel projects past the square. Stitch.

3 Stitching panel ends With right sides together, pin the short ends of each side panel to the remaining long edge of the one before. Stitch seams, then press them open.

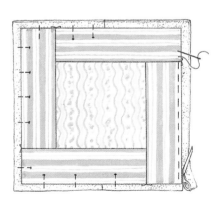

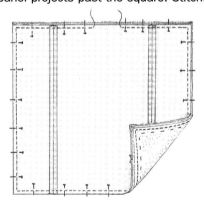

4 Adding wadding Join the two widths of wadding by butting the edges and oversewing them. Pin the wrong side of the throw to wadding, trimming away any excess. Tack round the edges through both layers.

5 Adding backing Make up backing by joining two panels on either side of the width, then trim to size. Right sides together, pin throw front to backing, and stitch all round, leaving a 20cm (8in) gap for turning. Trim corners, then turn to right side and press. Slipstitch gap closed.

6 Completing throw Pin, then stitch the trim all round the edge, mitring it at the corners and overlapping the ends neatly. Using double thread and stitching through all layers, attach one button in the centre. Space the other four buttons equally towards each corner of the centre panel and stitch.

Bed corona

Curtains flowing down on either side of the bedhead – from a circlet of track or a corona fixed above the bed – are guaranteed to give your bedroom a wonderfully romantic look.

A corona is a small, half-moon shaped track fixed to the wall above the head of the bed to carry a pair of curtains that cascade down to the floor on each side. The drapes are generally caught back into tiebacks or holdbacks at headboard height to clear the pillows and exaggerate the graceful sweep of the fabric.

Unlined curtains look simple and elegant, or you can add a contrasting lining to set off the decorating scheme in your bedroom. For a really sumptuous effect, continue the curtaining behind the bedhead by adding a head curtain in the contrast lining. To vary the effect, you can also experiment with different curtain headings or add a pretty valance.

You can match the bed curtains with your window treatment or bedlinen for a unified effect. Many fabric ranges include coordinated sheeting in plain colours, and florals, stripes and checks

▲ *Choose fabrics for your corona curtains to link with the surrounding decor – in this case green painted coving, a floral frieze and matching bed cushions.*

which you can use as curtain lining.

By crowning the bed with delicate lace or voile drapes, you can create a young girl's dream bed; or go for film-star glamour with luxurious folds of taffeta or satin. Choose tassel tiebacks, or make matching fabric tiebacks.

Fixing the track and tieback hooks

There are a number of corona kits available in department stores and do-it-yourself superstores which provide all the fittings required to give a firm support for the bed drapes.

A kit should include:
◆ Half-moon shaped track
◆ Wall brackets, screws and wallplugs
◆ Tieback hooks and wallplugs
◆ Curtain runners
◆ Valance hooks (optional)

1 Positioning the corona Decide on the position of the corona above the head of the bed. About 213cm (7ft) is usual but you may wish to vary this according to the ceiling height and bed size.

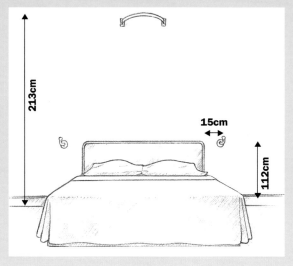

2 Fixing the corona Assemble the corona and fix it centrally over the bed at the desired height, following the manufacturer's instructions carefully.

3 Fixing tieback hooks Position and fix the tieback hooks level with the top of the headboard or 112cm (44in) from the floor, and 12.5-15cm (5-6in) out from each side of the bed.

Making unlined corona side curtains

The side curtains are each made from one width of furnishing fabric, 120-140cm (48-54in) wide. For a fuller effect, add a half width to each curtain on the edge nearest the wall.

1 Measuring up and cutting Tie one end of the string to the track, loop it over the tieback hook in a gentle curve, then let it hang to the floor. Mark the string with sticky tape where it hits the floor. Measure the string from the track to the tape and add 16cm (6¼in) for heading and hem. Cut two widths of fabric to this length.

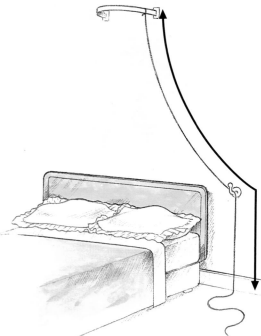

2 Hemming the sides and base To make each curtain, press under a double 1.5cm (⅝in) hem on each selvedge and machine stitch. At the base edge, press under a double 5cm (2in) hem and stitch.

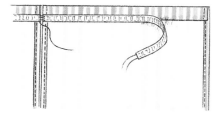

3 Making the heading Press under a 6cm (2¼in) turning along the top edge. Position the tape to cover the raw edge by 1.5cm (⅝in) and stitch. Lay the two curtains side by side and firmly oversew the leading edges together at the heading tape.

You will need

◆ Bed corona kit
◆ Furnishing fabric
◆ Heading tape
◆ One pair of tiebacks
◆ Drill and screwdriver
◆ Length of string or cord
◆ Tape measure
◆ Scissors, pins and needle
◆ Matching sewing thread

4 Hanging the curtains Pull up the tapes to fit the track and insert the hooks. Hang the curtains in place, looping them out to the tiebacks, with extra fullness at the leading edge so the hem falls in a pretty tail.

Tip

HIDDEN TRACK
To create an attractive frilled effect on the curtain top, attach the tape 2-3cm (1-1½in) down from the top.

Making lined corona side curtains

Lining your corona curtains gives you the scope to choose two different fabrics to complement your scheme, and to use pretty, lightweight prints which look better lined. The lining is easy to attach because it is 'bagged out'; this means the main fabric and lining pieces are cut to the same size, so that when they are joined and turned right way out the lining comes to the edge of the curtain at the sides and base. Buy the same amount of lining as main fabric.

1 **Measuring and cutting** Measure the drop as in step **1** opposite, but add only 7.5cm (3in) for turnings. Cut two widths of curtain fabric this length, then two in lining fabric.

▲ *A pastel print in similar tones to the walls is a pretty, restful choice for unlined corona drapes. Brass holdbacks to match the bedstead hold the curtains in place.*

2 **Making up** Right sides together, pin one piece of lining fabric to one piece of curtain fabric. Stitch down the sides and along the hem, taking a 1.5cm (⅝in) seam allowance. Clip the corners of the seam allowances, and turn right side out. Press well, taking care that the seamlines sit along the edges of the curtain.

3 **Completing the curtains** Continue as in steps **3** and **4** opposite, treating the two layers as one.

Corona head curtain

A corona head curtain is hung on the wall behind the bed, filling the space between the side curtains and creating an attractive backdrop. The curtain is unlined and hung with the right side facing out. It is caught to the tieback hooks at the sides with curtain rings. Use one width of fabric for a single bed, and two for a double. Choose fabric to match the side curtain lining, if any.

Some corona kits include track across the back of the corona for the head curtain; otherwise you need to fix a short length of light track to the wall between the corona brackets. Fix this track at the same height as the corona track.

You will need

- ◆ Curtain fabric
- ◆ Heading tape
- ◆ Matching thread
- ◆ Two curtain rings

1 Cutting and joining Cut one or two widths of fabric (according to bed size), the length of the measuring-up string plus 6cm (2¼in). If using two widths, split one width into two half widths, and join one on either side of the full width, with right sides together. Press the seams open.

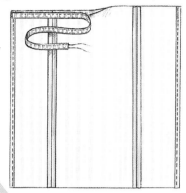

2 Finishing the sides and top Press under and stitch a double 1cm (⅜in) hem on each side edge. At the top edge, press under a 4cm (1½in) turning, and position the tape so that it covers the raw edge by 1cm (⅜in). Stitch the tape on and pull up the gathers to fit the track.

3 Hanging the curtain Hang all the curtains in place. Drape the side curtains as in step **4**, *Making unlined corona side curtains.* Following the line of the side curtains, draw each side edge of the head curtain out to the hooks, and stitch a curtain ring at this point. Put the rings over the hooks.

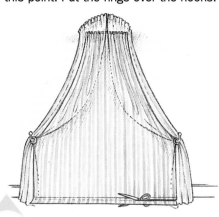

4 Hemming the curtain Mark a line along the base edge of the curtain, 2cm (¾in) beyond floor level, and trim along this line. Take the curtain down. Press then stitch a double 1cm (⅜in) hem. Rehang the curtain on the track and attach to the tieback hooks.

Corona valance

A gathered valance tops off your corona in grand style, matching it to the window dressing or adding a flourish to a plain room. When crowning your bed drapes with a valance, make the side curtains without a top frill as the track is hidden by the valance.

Making the valance Make the lined or unlined valance, using two widths of fabric and adapting the length to suit the proportions of your corona drapes – as a guide, 30cm (12in) is usually a good length. Hang the valance in place using valance hooks which clip on to the track – these may be supplied with your corona kit; if not, buy them to fit your track.

▶A corona valance in fabric to match the upholstered headboard makes an impressive crown for sheer bed drapes and balances the overall effect. Matching fabric rosettes attached to the stem holdbacks make charming details.

Guest room daybed

Pamper your guests and spoil yourself with a versatile and elegant daybed. It makes a luxurious setting for an overnight stay, but can also provide an enticing retreat during the day.

Placing a single bed against a wall makes the most of a small space, and a graceful and airy voile drape gives it impact and importance. With a formal bedcover, bolsters and pillow shams you can turn a bedroom into a useful sitting room for daytime use.

You can make this arrangement with any bed which has both head and foot boards – it looks best if they are both roughly the same height. Secondhand brass or wooden bedsteads are ideal, but if you can't find what you want, it's easy to add bed ends to a single bed. Fit sturdy trellis panels to the end of the bed, or buy willow hurdles from garden suppliers to make the end boards.

The ensemble featured here is made from a mixture of formal checks and stripes to set off the softly flowered voile; the colours are pretty but fresh. For a pale, neutral colour scheme, use a combination of textures in natural creams and beiges, with touches of soft cherry red and a drape of spotted voile. Or give the room a contemporary twist with rich terracotta voile and plain cottons and linens in indigo and mauve.

▲ *A graceful swoop of voile complements the scalloped edging of a crisply cut fitted bedcover. Piping and bobble edging in a contrasting shade of red add subtle detail and accentuate the delicate yellow print of the fabric.*

...g the bedcover

...er has piping round the top
... side and end panels are cut
scr... .y, with the end panels falling
down between the mattress and the
boards to continue the line below. If
you are making the bedcover for a bed

with solid head and foot boards, all you
need is a short flap at each end, which
you can tuck down between the board
and the mattress, as the end panels will
be hidden. The side panels are faced
with the same fabric as the bedcover.

You will need

- ◆ **Furnishing fabric**
- ◆ **Lining fabric**
- ◆ **Contrast fabric for piping**
- ◆ **Piping cord**
- ◆ **Matching thread**
- ◆ **Paper and pencil**
- ◆ **Pins**
- ◆ **Tape measure**
- ◆ **Flexible curve (optional)**

1 Measuring up Measure the
length of the bed
base between the
boards (**A**) and
the width (**B**). Then
measure the width
of the bed between
the end posts (**C**).
Finally, decide on
the total depth of
the side and end
panels (**D**).

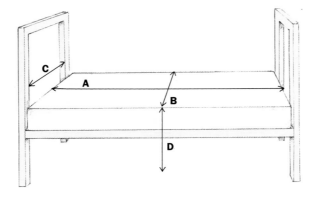

2 Cutting the top panel *For the top panel:* adding 3cm
(1¼in) to both **A** and **B**, cut a piece of furnishing fabric
to this measurement. *For the lining:* repeat to cut a piece
of lining fabric to the same size.

3 Cutting the side panels *For the side panels:* add
3cm (1¼in) to **A**, then cut enough widths of fabric to
measure **D** plus 3cm (1¼in) deep to make four panels to
this measurement. *For the end panels:* add 3cm (1¼in) to
C and cut four pieces to this measurement across the
width of the fabric, by **D** plus 3cm (1¼in).

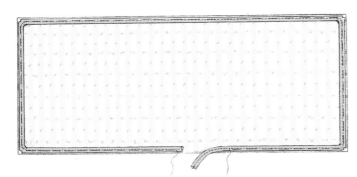

4 Piping the top edge Cut and make up enough piping
from contrasting fabric to go round all four sides of the
top panel. Using a zip foot or half foot on your sewing
machine, apply piping to top panel edges, pivoting the
needle at the corners.

5 Cutting scallop template
Divide **A** equally into about
26-30cm (10-12in) divisions.
Cut a piece of paper to this
width by the depth of **D**. On
each long side, mark 10cm
(4in) up from the bottom
edge, then fold the paper in
half down the length. Using a
flexible curve or household
object, draw a curve from the
side mark to the folded
bottom edge; cut along curve.

6 Joining side panels Right sides together, join widths
to make up side panels and self-facings; press seams
open. Right sides together, pin each panel to its facing.

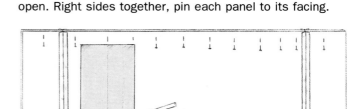

7 Shaping the scallops On one end of a side panel, with
facing side down, position the template 1.5cm (⅝in) in
from the side edge, with the curve 1.5cm (⅝in) up from
the bottom edge. Draw round the curve, then move the
template along to the end of the curve. Repeat to end.

8 Stitching the scallops Stitch down one side edge,
along the scallop curves and up the other side edge.
Trim the seam allowances and clip corners and into
curves. Turn panel to right side and press; then tack
along the top edge. Repeat with the other side panel.

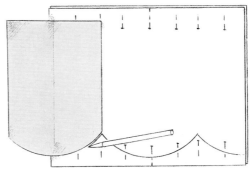

9 Shaping the end panels Pin each end panel and its
self-facing right sides together. Mark the centre of one
panel and centre the template on it, with the curve 1.5cm
(⅝in) up from the bottom edge. Draw in the curve, then
move the template and continue on either side to the
edges – there may be part scallops at either end. Repeat
with the other end panel. Stitch as for the side panels.

Combine checks, stripes and florals to create an interesting and harmonious scheme for a day bed. This bed provides the perfect escape in which to relax and put your feet up for a few moments.

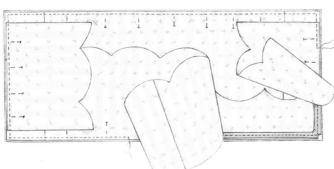

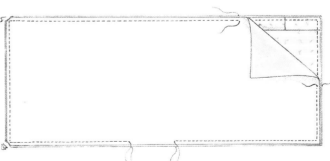

10 Putting the cover together With the right sides and raw edges together, pin the side panels to the side edges of the top panel, sandwiching the piping between. Then centre and pin the end panels to the head and foot ends. Stitch all round.

11 Lining the top panel With right sides and raw edges together, and with the side panels folded in, pin the lining to the top panel. Stitch, leaving a 20cm (8in) opening for turning through. Trim and layer the seam allowances, then turn to right side. Slipstitch the opening closed and press.

Making the bed drape

The bed drape is very simply made from a single width of fabric, with a casing stitched in the centre and a decorative trim along one side edge and both ends. The drape hangs from a rod or pole which is anchored at a right angle to the wall. This is fixed with a dowel screw – a headless screw with a thread at both ends, available from hardware stores.

1 **Preparing the pole** Cut the pole 45cm (18in) long. Re-drill the hole in the cut end, then screw in the double-threaded screw. Drill and plug a hole for the screw directly above the centre of the bed at the chosen height – about 213cm (7ft) is usual.

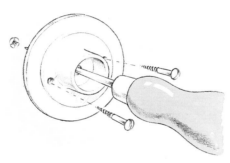

2 **Fixing the bracket** Drill a small hole through the centre of the bracket so that you can centre it over the hole using a bradawl. Fix the bracket in place with the screws supplied. Screw in the dowel screw at the end of the pole, through the centre hole in the fixing bracket and into the wall.

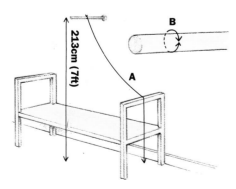

3 **Measuring up** Tie a long piece of string to the pole and drape it over one end of the bed, to finish 5-7.5cm (2-3in) above the floor. Measure the length of the string (**A**). Then measure loosely round the pole (**B**).

The pole is also supported by a recess bracket. If you find you are unable to buy the components separately, then buy the shortest pole kit available plus one recess bracket. Alternatively, you can use a large decorative bracket, such as one which supports hanging baskets; add a pretty posy of fabric rosebuds and leaves to conceal the projecting end.

4 **Preparing fabric** From one end of the length of fabric, measure and mark **A**, then **B**, then **A** again, adding 2cm (¾in). Cut off surplus fabric beyond this point. On all four sides, press under a double 1cm (⅜in) hem. Stitch long back edge only.

5 **Stitching the trim** On the right side and starting at a lower back corner, pin the trim along the short end of the fabric, laying it on top of the pressed hem and turning in the cut end. Continue along the long front edge, then the other short end, mitring the corners. Stitch, catching in the pressed hem at the same time.

6 **Making the casing** Fold the drape in half across the length, with the wrong sides together and matching the **B** marks. Pin, then stitch across the drape at this point, making sure it is parallel to the centre fold. Gently thread the casing on to the pole and screw on the finial.

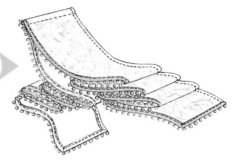

Transform a small guest room into a warm and inviting seating area for daytime by adding coordinating bolsters and shams to a stylish bedcover and bed drape.

Guest room cushions

*Placing a bolster at each end of a single bed transforms it
into an elegant sofa. These cleverly styled bolsters and matching
pillow shams echo the scalloped detail of the bedcover.*

Prettily styled accessories adorned with fine detail display fabrics at their best, and can give a single bed a thoroughly well-dressed look for daytime use. Push the bed against the wall, and place a bolster at each end to give it the neat, structured look of a sofa; slip the coordinating pillow shams over ordinary pillows to turn them into elegant cushions for extra comfort.

The bolster has beautifully scalloped ends, and buttons neatly together along its length. Choose a contrasting fabric for the end circles and make the most of the buttoning detail with large fabric-covered buttons, or decorative novelty buttons in flower shapes.

The delicate shaping of the pillow sham is accentuated with fine piping, and the inner seam is satin-stitched for a smart, professional-looking finish.

The undulating curves of scalloped edges add a touch of old-fashioned charm to a plump, buttoned bolster and a pair of pillows. Fine contrast piping highlights the wavy outlines of the pillow shams.

Making the bolster

You need a bolster pad about 7.5cm (3in) shorter than the width of the bed, and roughly 20cm (8in) in diameter. For the cover, choose mediumweight, firmly woven furnishing fabrics.

1 Measuring up Measure the diameter (**A**), the circumference (**B**) and the length of the bolster (**C**).

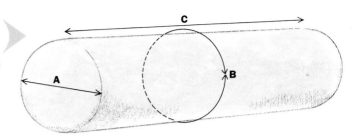

You will need

◆ Bolster pad

◆ Fabric for main section and facings

◆ Contrast fabric for end sections

◆ Matching thread

◆ Four self-cover buttons

◆ Paper for template

◆ Tape measure

◆ Pencil

◆ Dressmaker's pencil

◆ Needle and thread

◆ Zipper or half machine foot

2 Cutting out *For the main section:* cut one piece **C** plus 10cm (4in) by **B** plus 15cm (6in). *For the scallop facings:* with the pattern running in the same direction as the main section, cut two strips **B** plus 3cm (1¼) by 6cm (2¼in).

3 Cutting the end circles Make a circular paper pattern with a radius of ½ **A** plus 1.5cm (⅝in). Use the pattern to cut two circles in contrast fabric.

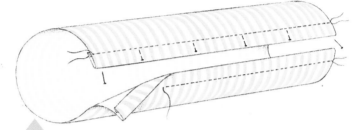

4 Hemming the main section On the top and bottom edges of the main section, press under 1cm (⅜in) then 4cm (1½in). Stitch close to the inner fold. On the right side of one hemmed edge, place a pin 5cm (2in) in from each end; divide the space between into five equal sections and mark with pins. Remove the first two pins.

▶ *Pick out a colour from the main fabric for the end circle of the bolster. The yellow textured weave shown here matches the pillows and echoes the yellow in the stripe, while the buttons feature the tiny floral sprig from the bedcover.*

5 Working the buttonholes Using matching thread, work a buttonhole at each pin mark; set the buttonholes at right angles to the hem and 1cm (⅜in) in from the edge.

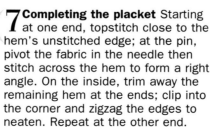

6 Starting the placket Right side out, lap the buttonholed hem edge over the other hem by the hem depth; pin at each end. Then, 5cm (2in) from each end, place a pin at right angles to the hem edge.

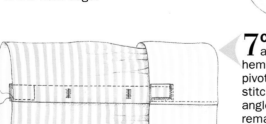

7 Completing the placket Starting at one end, topstitch close to the hem's unstitched edge; at the pin, pivot the fabric in the needle then stitch across the hem to form a right angle. On the inside, trim away the remaining hem at the ends; clip into the corner and zigzag the edges to neaten. Repeat at the other end.

8 Making a scallop template Divide circumference **B** into equal sections of 6-9cm (2¼-3½in). Cut a piece of paper this height by 6cm (2¼in) deep. Mark centre of bottom edge, and mark each side edge 2cm (¾in) up. Draw a curve from side edges through centre mark. Cut out.

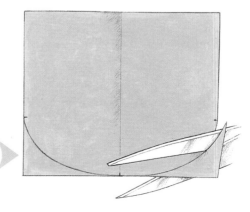

11 **Attaching the facings** Right sides together, pin a facing to each end of the main section, with the curved facing edges level with raw edge of main section. Stitch carefully 1.5cm (⅝in) in from the facing edge.

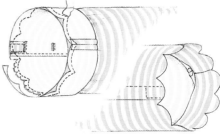

12 **Turning the facing** Trim and clip the seam allowances. Turn each facing to the inside, carefully pushing out the shaping, and press.

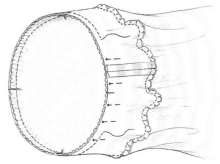

13 **Adding the end circles** Turn the cover inside out and open out the facings. Divide the raw edges of the facings and end circles into four and mark. Right sides together, and matching raw edges and marks, pin a circle into each facing. Stitch.

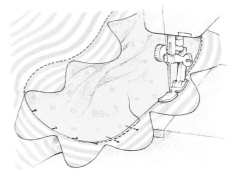

14 **Securing the facings** Turn cover right side out and push the facings back into place inside the cover; pin. Using a zip foot or half foot on your machine, stitch round through the main section and facing, close to the seamline at each end.

15 **Completing the cover** On the inside, trim and zigzag stitch the end seams. Sew on the buttons to correspond with the buttonholes. Insert the pad, and fasten the buttons.

9 **Marking the scallops** On the wrong side of a facing strip, place the template 1.5cm (⅝in) from one short edge, with the base of curve on lower raw edge; draw round the curve. Move along and mark in the next curve. Continue like this, finishing 1.5cm (⅝in) from the end.

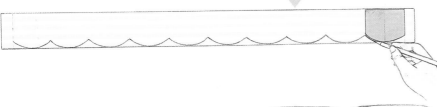

10 **Making the end facings** Lay the two facing strips together and cut along the marked line through both layers. Separate the strips. Right sides together, match the short ends of one strip to make a loop. Pin; stitch, and press the seams open. Repeat for the other strip.

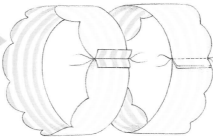

Making the pillow sham

These attractive pillow shams dress the bed smartly for daytime use. The edges are daintily scalloped, and fine contrast piping picks out the shaping – size 2 or 3 piping cord is ideal.

The instructions are for a standard pillow measuring 71 x 46cm (28 x 18in); for a pillow of a different size, you need to find a scallop size that fits exactly into both edge measurements.

You will need

For one standard pillow:

◆ **1.2m (1⅜yd) fabric**

◆ **Fabric for piping**

◆ **4m (4⅜yd) fine piping cord**

◆ **Matching thread**

◆ **Paper for pattern**

◆ **Piping foot for machine**

Fine piping and a row of satin stitch makes the most of colour contrasts and gives a crisp, tailored finish to the pillows.

1 Cutting out Cut out the front and back pieces, following step **1** on page 106.

2 Cutting the template Cut a piece of paper 8.3cm (3⅜in) wide and 6.5cm (2½in) deep. Mark the centre of the long lower edge, and 2cm (¾in) up from base edge at each side edge. Draw and cut out a scallop template, as in step **8** on page 120.

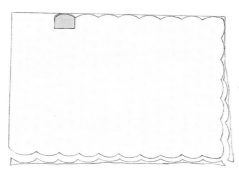

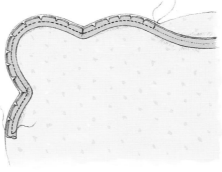

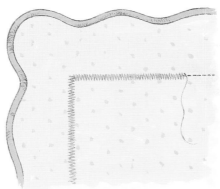

3 Marking the scallops Lay out the front piece wrong side up. Place the template on one corner, with the curve on the raw edge and the side edges matching. Draw round shape and move on, continuing all round. At corners, make a smooth line where the scallops overlap. Adjust to fit if necessary. Cut along scalloped edge.

4 Applying the piping Make up the piping and apply carefully all round the scalloped edge, clipping the piping seam allowances as you go.

5 Assembling the sham Hem the back sections and join the front and backs, as on page 106, steps **3-4**, carefully following previous stitching line of the scallops.

6 Finishing off Trim and clip the seam allowances carefully, then turn the cover to the right side and press. Pin all round 5cm (2in) from the outer edge. Using thread to match the piping, stitch along pinned line. Set your machine to a medium width satin stitch, and stitch over the line of straight stitches.

Guest room accessories

Delicately tinted muslin brings a romantic softness to the bedroom.
Use it to make an intricately pleated and rose trimmed nightdress
case, and appliquéd in leafy sprays on bedlinen.

An unashamedly feminine nightdress case will rest gracefully on the bed – hinting at glamour and luxury, but without any unnecessary frills and flounces. The nightdress case looks soft and dainty in muslin or Swiss voile, but you can also make it in fine silk or satin – the folds will show off the gleam of the silky fabric beautifully. The pleated section is lined so that it will always keep its shape. The tiny fabric roses and leaves are lightly padded to give them a full, squashy plumpness.

A touch of leafy green adds a springlike freshness to crisp white bedlinen, and turns a plain sheet and pillowcase into a bedroom set to be proud of. If you want to, you can apply the design to the duvet cover as well. This simple design has a rolling stem of pearl cotton thread, stitched down with machine zigzag. Dainty muslin leaves are appliquéd along its length, and you can add just a single spray, or set sprays end to end to make a continuous trim. Or you can fill the corners with several sprays originating from one point for a 'fan' effect. The design is incredibly versatile, so create your own pattern to suit your taste.

◀ *A simple design of leaves on an undulating stem makes a pretty appliqué for bedlinen. Work it in soft muslin for a delicate effect.*

Making the nightdress case

Choose a fine, slightly translucent fabric for the nightdress case; for the lining use a toning fabric with a firmer weave, such as calico or furnishing cotton. The fabric is pleated freehand, directly on to the lining, and then cut to shape, so make sure you can see the outline of the lining square through the fabric as you pleat. Don't worry about making the pleats completely equal and evenly spaced – a soft unstructured look is much prettier. You can overlap the narrow converging pleats at the top corner as they'll be hidden by the roses.

You will need

- ◆ **1.5m (1⅝yd) fine fabric**
- ◆ **0.4m (½yd) lining fabric**
- ◆ **Scraps contrast fabric for roses and leaves**
- ◆ **Matching threads**
- ◆ **Scraps of wadding for roses and leaves**

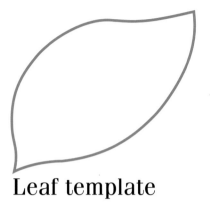

Leaf template

1 Cutting out *For the front:* cut a 100 x 60 cm (39½ x 23½in) rectangle of fine fabric. *For the back:* from fine fabric, cut one 33cm (13in) square and one 33 x 13cm (13 x 5⅛in) rectangle. Turn under 3mm (⅛in) then 6mm (¼in) on one edge of each of these. Press and stitch. *For the lining:* cut one 33cm (13in) square of lining fabric.

2 Preparing to pleat Place the lining square wrong side up on the work surface. On the front fabric piece, mark the centre of one long edge – this will be the top edge. Lay it wrong side down over the lining, matching the top edges and with the centre mark about 2.5cm (1in) in from the right hand edge of the lining square. Pin along the top edge.

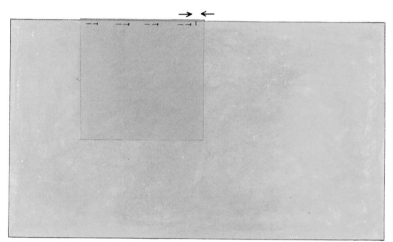

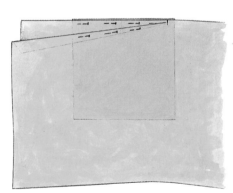

3 Starting the pleats On left edge of the fabric, pinch a pleat about 2.5cm (1in) deep; angle the pleat so that it points towards the centre mark and narrows to about 0.5cm (¼in) at the top edge. Pin in place.

4 Completing the pleats Move down the fabric edge for about 5cm (2in) and make another pleat like the first, so the two pleats converge on the centre point. Continue in this way round the side and along the adjacent edge of the fabric, making eight to ten pleats in all.

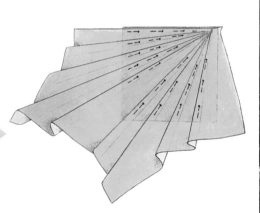

5 Securing the pleats When you are satisfied that all the pleats are lying smoothly, tack all round the edge of the lining and front piece. Turn the work over and trim the excess fabric which is level with the lining square.

6 Assembling the cover Lay out front, lining side down. Right sides down and matching raw edges, lay back pieces on top, hemmed edges overlapping. Stitch round all sides. Zigzag stitch edge. Turn out; press.

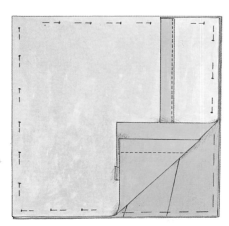

◄ *Softly pleated voile radiating from a posy of rosebuds makes a magical nightdress case for a special guest.*

7 **Making the roses** *From voile:* cut a 30 x 8cm (12 x 3¼in) bias strip. *From wadding:* cut a 30 x 4cm (12 x 1½in) strip. Fold voile in half lengthways round wadding, and trim curves at each end. Using double thread, knotted at the end, stitch 6mm (¼in) from the edge and loosely gather. Roll up three turns tightly and stitch through to secure. Continue to roll less tightly but pulling the gathers more closely. Stitch through the base to secure as you go and work a few firm backstitches when rolled.

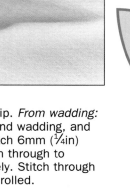

8 **Making the leaves** Using the leaf template on page 124, and leaving a margin all round, cut two leaves from contrast fabric and one from wadding. Sandwich the wadding leaf between the fabric leaves, and work close satin stitch along centre of leaf, and around leaf outline through all layers. Trim close to stitching. Repeat for two more leaves.

9 **Attaching the trim** Arrange the roses and leaves in a posy over the pleating at the top corner of the nightdress case. Stitch in place with small stitches, taking care not to catch the back sections.

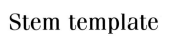

Stem template

Leafy bedlinen

Subtly varied shades of the same colour add interest and depth to the design. The stem here is made from three strands of pearl cotton embroidery thread, but you can get the same effect with fine cord. Choose a matching sewing thread for the zigzag and another shade which contrasts with the leaf fabric so that the satin-stitched stem and outline show up well. You can use any soft, fine fabric in plains or small patterns for the leaves.

The appliqué will fit the standard 5cm (2in) wide sheet hem or Oxford pillowcase border. If the sheet has a narrower hem, make a new 5cm (2in) hem on the other end instead, using one of the coloured threads so the stitching is part of the design. On a housewife pillowcase, position one spray across a corner, or parallel with the opening.

▶ *Set the spray end to end to run continuously along the edge of the bedlinen, or just position a single spray at one corner for a more subtle decoration.*

1 **Tracing the design** Trace the design from previous page on to tracing paper and cut it out.

You will need

- ◆ **Set of bedlinen**
- ◆ **Pearl cotton embroidery thread or fine cord**
- ◆ **Scraps of muslin or other fine fabric**
- ◆ **Bonding fabric such as Bondaweb**
- ◆ **Sewing threads to contrast slightly with fabric and embroidery thread**
- ◆ **Tracing paper**
- ◆ **Masking tape**
- ◆ **Dressmaker's carbon paper**
- ◆ **Cording machine foot**

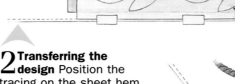

2 **Transferring the design** Position the tracing on the sheet hem or the top opening edge of the pillowcase and transfer it. Move the tracing along and repeat for a continuous trim.

3 **Working the stem** Measure along the stem and add one-third again. Cut three strands of pearl cotton to this measurement and twist them together lightly; alternatively cut one piece of fine cord. Lay the cord or twisted threads along the stem line. Fit the cording machine foot, and set the machine to medium width zigzag stitch. Securing the ends with a number of stitches, zigzag over the threads, following the traced line.

4 **Bonding the motifs** Using the leaves on the tracing paper as patterns, back the leaves with the bonding fabric and fuse them in position.

5 **Working the appliqué** Zigzag stitch then satin stitch the leaves in place, varying the stitch width from thick to thin, according to the leaf shape.

Index

Picture Acknowledgements

Photographs: 7 Robert Harding Syndication/Homes and Gardens/Jan Baldwin, 8-9 Eaglemoss/Lizzie Orme, 9(t) Textra, (br) Osborne and Little, 10 Harlequin, 11 Ariadne, Holland, 13 Marie Claire IdÈes/Bouquet/Lancrenon, 15 Eaglemoss/Adrian Taylor, 16 Ariadne Holland, 17 rhs/ipc/Woman and Home, 18-20 Eaglemoss/Lizzie Orme, 21-24 Biggie Best, 25 Eaglemoss/Steve Tanner, 26 Romo, 27 Eaglemoss/Graham Rae, 28-30 Eaglemoss/Steve Tanner, 31 Robert Harding Syndication/IPC Magazines/Ideal Home, 33 Robert Harding Syndication/IPC Magazines/Homes and Gardens, 34 Integra Products, 35-38 Eaglemoss/Willy Camden, 39 Robert Harding Syndication/Ideal Home/Brian Harrison, 41 Robert Harding Syndication/Ideal Home/Dominic Blackmore, 42 Robert Harding Syndication/Homes and Gardens/Hugh Johnson, 43 Robert Harding Syndication/IPC Magazines/Country Homes and Interiors, 44-5 Eaglemoss/Lizzie Orme, 46 rhs/ipc/Woman's Journal, 47 Robert Harding Syndication/IPC Magazines/Homes and Gardens, 48 Robert Harding Syndication/IPC Magazines/Ideal Home, 49 Elizabeth Whiting and Associates/James Merrel, 51 Harris Fabrics, 52 Harrison Drape, 53 Eaglemoss/Lizzie Orme, 57, 59 Robert Harding Syndication/IPC Magazines/Homes and Gardens, 60 Laura Ashley, 61 Elizabeth Whiting and Associates/Peter Woloszinski, 63 Robert Harding Syndication/Homes and Ideas/Dominic Blackmore, 64 Robert Harding Syndication/Homes and Gardens/Russell Sadur, 65 Doehet Zelf, 66, 68 Ariadne, Holland, 69 Robert Harding Syndication/IPC Magazines/Homes and Gardens, 70-72 Ariadne, Holland, 73 Elizabeth Whiting and Associates/Rodney Hyett, 74-75 Eaglemoss/Simon Page-Ritchie, 76 Crowson Fabrics, 77 Ariadne, Holland, 78-79 Eaglemoss/Lizzie Orme, 79(t) Ariadne, Holland, 80 Robert Harding Syndication/IPC Magazines/Homes and Gardens, 81-82 Eaglemoss/Lizzie Orme, 83 Worldwide Syndication, 84-85 Robert Harding Syndication/IPC Magazines/Ideal Home, 86 Worldwide Syndication, 89-95 Eaglemoss/Lizzie Orme, 96 Eaglemoss/Simon Page-Ritchie, 97-110 Eaglemoss/Lizzie Orme, 111 Robert Harding Syndication/IPC Magazines, 112 Graham Nash, 113 Rufflette, 114 Elizabeth Whiting and Associates/Andreas von Einsiedel, 115-122 Eaglemoss/Lizzie Orme, 123-126 Eaglemoss.

Illustrations: 87-88 Coral Mula. All others John Hutchinson.